Timeless Top 10 Travel Guides

Rome

Top 10 Districts, Shopping and Dining, Museums, Activities, Historical Sights, Nightlife, Top Things to do Off the Beaten Path, and Much More!

By Tess Downey

Foreword

Christianity and the Roman Empire are the two main factors that put Italy "on the map" – forever. Rome, the country's capital, is not just any other historical city – in fact, it even goes beyond history. It is actually an understatement to say that the city of Rome played a crucial part in all of humanity because in one way or another it gave birth to the modern day society we came to know. Needless to say, Rome is not just part of history, this very city single – handedly created the beginning of history itself.

Forget Paris, forget Greece, forget London and all of the other main European countries because before these "major cities" came about, before each of them made history on their own, there is only but one empire that propelled human civilization forward and somewhat influenced different nations to make their own marks in the world.

Embark on a phenomenal journey and find out why Rome is the birth place of the greatest civilization in human history.

Table of Contents

Introduction

Rome, also known as the "Eternal City," is filled with nothing but history and legacy. It is the home of the Vatican where the highest leader of the Catholic Church resides, and it is still the cultural and historical center of the world.

Rome is famously known for being the city that gave birth to perhaps the greatest civilization in human history – the Roman Empire. This is the place where it all began – the faith, the government, the modern day society, the traditions, the customs and culture, the art, the law, the way of life and everything that you can possibly imagine – the Romans one way or another influenced us all.

If you decide to visit this place, you will never run out of things to discover because the city is like a feast of endless courses! Even if you think you have seen it all, you will never feel like you've even scratch the surface. No matter how many times you come back, and even if you grew up in this place, everything you see will always just be a tip of the iceberg.

It's no surprise that the imperial glory days of Rome still echoes in the modern day era, if you think about it, there are a lot of other empires and ancient civilizations who have also made its mark in the world but what makes Rome and the Roman Empire different? Why is this place the residential of the Papacy – and not Jerusalem? Why do people, despite of the horror that this civilization brought about, let their lives be influenced by it? Why do we regard the empire as the greatest in history?

We may never know the exact answer for sure because there are many reasons and factors that will come into play, even if you ask a scholar or a historian who have spent their whole lives studying this civilization they may not give you the answer you are looking for – but one thing's for sure – the Romans have contributed so much that it's just impossible not to remember them at all.

Whether this is your first time to visit the Eternal City or not there's always something new and different to see. The frontiers of the Roman Empire go beyond the city of Rome itself. Rome's power and splendor are displayed in the way we live our lives today – from the golden days of the ancient empire to the establishment of the Renaissance, Rome is still a living and breathing masterpiece!

In this book, you will learn the basic things you need to know about Rome: its world – renowned location, its historical people, its language, culture and traditions. You will also be given information regarding your travel needs, and of course an overview of the top tourist attractions, districts and food places as well as hidden facets of the city to meet your thirst for exploration.

Let's go back in time to the city that started it all – All Roads Lead to Rome!

Chapter One: Rome Overview

Before you set foot on the Eternal City, it is essential to know specific details of what you're about to deal with. Ancient Rome is founded upon seven hills and it is divided into districts that have survived to this day. The present day city has the remnants of its glorious past that set a blazing trail for its future. You might want to consider discovering facts about this awesome place (although I'm pretty sure you have already learned so much about it in school) so that you know what to expect before you go about in your itinerary and to avoid getting into trouble.

In this chapter, you will be provided with an overview of Rome – its city, language, culture, people, and of course history!

If you have enough knowledge about these things, you will not just enjoy and appreciate the richness of the city but also get to be prepared for a phenomenal trip down memory lane!

Rome in Focus

The city of Rome is situated on the river of Tiber in between the Apennine Mountains and the Tyrrhenian Sea. It was once the center of the Roman Empire that ruled over a vast territory from the north of Great Britain to Mesopotamia. The city continues to be the center for administrative affairs in the country. It is now home to the Prime Minister of the Italian Government along with other ministerial offices including the Papacy.

There are about 2 million Italians residing in its metropolitan area, and it is also home to about 4 million people today.

Once you get to the city centre, you will immediately be awe-inspired because literally every corner in the city is filled with history, art and culture. The modern day Romans or Italians have very well preserved all of ancient Rome's most important contributions; you can see it from their grandiose architecture down to their classic Italian cuisine.

The city boasts its majestic basilicas, grand palaces, ancient style houses and cramp streets that echo the medieval era. It's safe to say that the city is literally still stuck in the past not because of its ancient - looking monuments or landmarks but mainly because of its own people. The Romans still carried to this day their ancestor's way of life through preserving various religious and cultural traditions.

The occupied territories of the ancient Roman Empire are now part of the UNESCO World Heritage Site. If you tour around Rome, it will seem like you are walking in a life-size museum. Europe's finest scenery and its most dramatic moments in history are all preserved in this beautiful city.

From its ancient walls, Rome is slowly transforming itself to catch up with the advances of modern day technology. And although the city is not the go – to place for tech – savvy millennials it is still a hotspot for tourists around the world. People just can't resist the authentic Roman gastronomy, the amazing scenery, the historical landmarks, and the grand architectures that once built and protected the city. Rome may not play a huge part in the techy wave of the future, but it's glorious past will forever stand the test of time.

Let us not forget that whatever technology we have today whether it is use in the battlefield, in transportation, in government, in gastronomy, in household, in the whole economy, even in the way we count, the way we number our days, the way we connect to the divine, and the way nations built an entire society is all because of the contributions of ancient Rome. Pretty much every little innovation that made our lives easier today can all be traced back to the city.

Perhaps this is the reason why people in the recent past, present and even the next generations regarded and will declare Rome as THE Eternal City. It's because without this once triumphant empire, the human race will never be where it is today if it wasn't for them. Rome literally built its city on rock and roll!

A Brief History of Rome

Before Rome was known as the Eternal City and before it became the hub of tourists all over the world it had gone through different phases and major changes; let's take a look at its colorful past so we can appreciate the city's present and look forward to its future.

- **753 BC: The Foundation of Rome**

  Romulus, one of the first seven Roman Kings, founded the city of Rome. Rome's original ancient name was Roma.

- **509 BC: Rome was established as a Republic**

  The Roman senators began ruling the city after they have expelled their last king. A constitution was set and the city became a republican government.

- **218 BC: Italian Invasion**

  Hannibal and his Carthage army attached and invaded Italy in the Second Punic War.

- **45 BC: The Rise of Julius Caesar and the invention of the Gregorian calendar**

  The Roman Republic ended after Julius Caesar conquered Pompeii in a civil war. Caesar became Rome's first ever dictator and supreme ruler. The new ruler hired an Egyptian astronomer to create a 12 month calendar that we now have today.

- **44 BC: The Fall of Julius Caesar**

  Marcus Brutus is assassinates Julius Caesar on the Ides of March with the hopes of bringing back the Roman Republic, unfortunately a civil war broke out instead.

- **27 BC: The Establishment of the Roman Empire**

  Octavius also known as Augustus appointed himself as Rome's first emperor.

- **64 A.D.: The attack of Nero**

  Nero burned the city and blamed the Christian for it. Nero eventually became Rome's notorious emperor.

- **80 A.D.: The Colosseum**

  The famous Colosseum was erected in 80 A.D. it was one of the first ever arena built in history. This is where gladiators fight to the death and was seen by thousands of Romans during that time.

- **122 AD: The Hadrian Wall is erected**

  The Hadrian Wall is one of the longest walls built during the time of the Romans that run across Northern Britain in order to keep the barbarians out

- **306 A.D.: The Rise of Emperor Constantine**

  Rome was a city known for persecuting Christians, but during Constantine's reign as emperor, the city transformed itself into a Christian empire.

- **380 A.D.: The Beginning of Christianity**

  In 380 A.D. Theodosius I proclaimed Christianity as the sole religion of the Roman Empire.

- **395 A.D.: The Division of Rome**

  The Roman Empire was split into two – the Eastern Roman Empire and the Western Roman Empire. It was divided by Theodosius.

- **410 A.D.: Visigoths Attack Rome**

  For the first time in 800 years, Rome had fallen to the enemy. The empire was attacked and conquered by Visigoths.

- **476 A.D.: The Fall of the Roman Empire**

  The last Roman Emperor Romulus Augustus was finally defeated by German Goth Odoacer; this marks the start of the Dark Ages in all of Europe.

- **1305 - 1420: Age of the Renaissance**

  During this time the papacy was transferred to Avignon, and only regained control around 1420. After Rome had declined, there was a rebuilding program at the forefront of the Renaissance. Pope Clement VII backed the French against Roman Emperor Charles V, Rome had fallen again which brought about it's yet another rebuilding.

- **1453: The End of the Byzantine Empire**

  The Ottoman Empire took over and the Byzantine era ends. The Ottoman Turks captured Constantinople. This part of the city was renamed Istanbul in 1930 which is now the capital of Turkey.

- **1808: Rome under Napoleon**

  French General Napoleon Bonaparte conquered the city and imprisoned the Pope.

- **1848 – 1871: Rome as Italy's Capital**

  In 1848, a revolution took place in the city, and a new Roman Republic was almost established. However, it was stopped by the French troops. The revolution eventually succeeded, and a new Kingdom of Italy was established. Soon the French troops left the country, and the Italian forces declared Rome as the capital of Italy in 1871.

- **1922 – 1933: The Rise and Fall of Benito Mussolini and the establishment of Vatican City**

  Benito Mussolini is one of Italy's famous dictators, and was a huge figure during the Second World War.

He marched his Blackshirts around 1922 which led to him taking control of Italy. In 1929, Vatican was declared as an independent state in Rome. Mussolini's regime eventually came to an end during the Second World War.

- **Present day Rome:** Rome is now inhabited with over 4 million residents, and visited by tourists and pilgrims from around the world. The Vatican City became the permanent residence of the Pope.

Rome's Language, People and Culture

I'm sure you've heard the saying that "when you're in Rome, do what the Romans are doing," well this is the perfect time to take that old adage literally.

Romanian's in general are very polite people; most of them will find a way to communicate to a visitor or a tourist like yourself, even if they don't speak your language. People, especially the elderly will surely appreciate old – fashioned politeness so you might want to address them as Mr. or Mrs. Handshaking is the most common gesture when greeting a fellow Romanian. You might want to also bring a gift if ever you are planning to visit an Italian friend. They will surely appreciate small gifts such as a flowers, chocolate or wine.

Rome's primary language is obviously Italian, but most of them – well at least the younger and middle – age generation – knows how to speak in English. The Roman dialect of varying degree is spoken among the older generations. Some people also speak Spanish, Latin, French and Portuguese since it has some similarities to the Italian language. As mentioned earlier, the city of Rome influenced the modern day society that we have today in many ways. You will definitely see it once you set foot on the city. In fact you can still trace the whole city back to the golden days of the Roman Empire.

If you look at the present day towns, forts and streets of Rome, you will see that this is the same frontier zone of the late empire. The structures, art and architecture of many places, including the materials used to build such monuments like cement, brick, mosaics, glass and wall paintings as well as columns and pillars that can be found in almost every structure in the world are all given to us by Ancient Rome.

A few more examples include the various inventions in the fields of engineering (roads, construction, sanitation), business (trade and commerce, concept of money, employment), government (constitution, laws, leadership), religion (Christianity, churches, the concept of God, rituals), Mathematics (Roman Numerals, Gregorian calendar), Art and Language (European languages, literature, communication, paintings, sculpture, theater), Recreation and Gastronomy (festivals, events, sports, spa, wine production) as well as Logistics, Military, and Transportation. They even invented the concept of marriage/weddings, the idea of contracts; properties, philosophies and almost everything in our way of life today are all rooted in Ancient Rome.

Rome was once the heartbeat of an empire, birthplace of one of the greatest civilizations on earth, it's the world's first metropolis inspired by ambition and driven by innovation. Written in stone, its ruins tell a remarkable story of a city and of a people who profoundly changed the world. There's only one word that could sum everything up about this city: it's Colossal. Perhaps the city's greatest feat is its endurance and supremacy that will last for centuries.

This isn't going to be one of those ordinary trips you may have had in the past, but one thing's for sure - this is one of those extraordinary trips you will surely remember in the future. The "City of God" is waiting for you!

Chapter Two: Travel Essentials

Now that you have learned several things about Rome and already have general knowledge of the city, the next thing for you to learn about and accomplish before actually going there is the travelling requirements or traveller's info.

The travel requirements and some basic reminders in planning your trip to this city are essential in order for you to have a wonderful experience and not get into trouble especially in immigration and customs.

In this chapter, you will learn what you need to do for you to be able to travel to Rome, Italy. You will learn the things you need to bring and be aware of as well as essential information for first time travellers such as money, and communication.

Visa and Passport Requirements

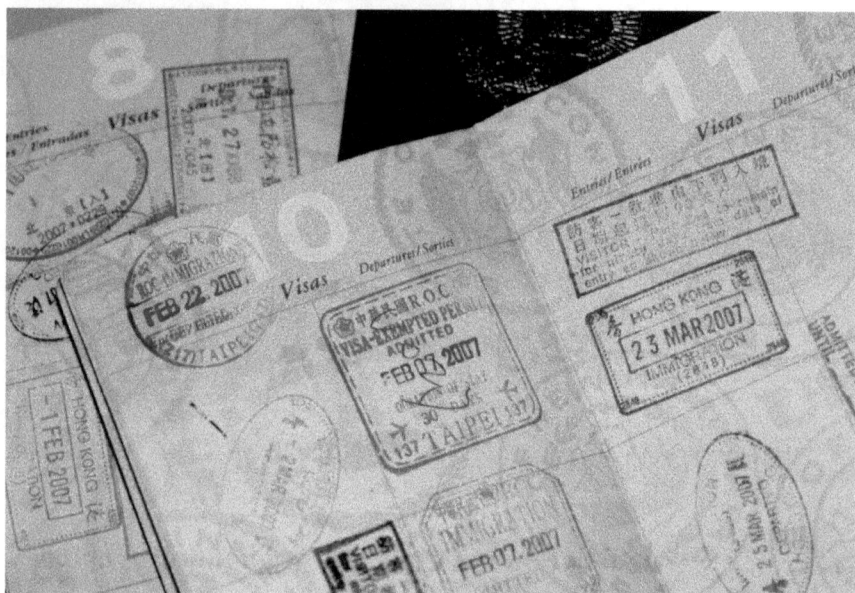

Just like other countries, a valid visa and updated passport is required for all visitors to the city. First and foremost, if you are a tourist, you need to have a passport with 6 months of validity.

American citizens as well as Australian, Switzerland and New Zealand citizens are not required to have a visa. For citizens of nations that is included in the European Union (EU), and European Economic Area (EEA) you are also not required to have a visa to enter the country. However, you should have a passport valid for 6 months from your departure date and you are only allowed to stay in the country for 90 days or 3 months.

If you are planning to stay longer in Italy for an extended vacation or other private matters, you may need to show proof that you have sufficient funds that will last you for your intended period. You may also be asked to show a confirmed onward and return flight tickets, and also the address of the place you're going to stay in/ hotel booking confirmation.

Aside from the countries mentioned above, here are the list of nations that are also allowed in Italy without a visa, same rules apply.

Below is the list of countries Yellow Fever Vaccination Certificate.

- Albania
- Andorra
- Antigua and Bermuda
- Argentina
- Bahamas
- Barbados
- Bosnia and Herzegovina
- Brazil
- Brunei
- Canada
- Chile
- Colombia
- Costa Rica
- Dominica
- East Timor
- Grenada

- Guatemala
- Honduras
- Israel
- Japan
- Macedonia
- Malaysia
- Mauritius
- Mexico
- Moldava
- Monaco
- Montenegro
- Nauru
- Nicaragua
- Panama
- Paraguay
- Peru
- Saint Kitts and Nevis
- Salvador
- Samoa
- Saint Lucia
- Saint Vincent and the Grenadines
- San Marino
- Serbia
- Seychelles
- Singapore
- South Korea
- Taiwan
- Tonga
- Trinidad and Tobago
- United Arab Emirates
- Uruguay
- Vanuatu
- Venezuela

For citizens of nations that are not included in the list mentioned above, you are required to acquire a Schengen Visa to enter Italy or even other countries that are part of the European Union. For more information, we recommend visiting the official website of the Ministry of Foreign Affairs of Italy.

Tourists and visitors should pass the Immigration and Security Checkpoints in various points of entry. Tourists are also not allowed to engage in any form of occupation, profession, business or any form of paid employment while in the country.

Traveller's Info

In this section, you will be provided with essential traveler's information on what to do and what not to do in Rome. Be sure to keep all these essentials in mind while you are traveling.

Money Exchange, ATMs, and Credit Cards

The currency in Rome is called Leu or Lei (pronounced as "lay"). The abbreviation of the currency is RON.

You can exchange your national money at various banks and exchanged offices in Rome (they are called *casa de schimb* or *birou de schimb valutar*). Of course you can also withdraw money on various ATMs where major debit cards are accepted. It can be found in almost all major attractions in the city, including the airport or other transportation hubs.

It is highly recommended that you exchange your money or withdraw notes right at the airport or in your hotels, so that it won't be too much hassle for you. It might also be a good idea to exchange large sums of money so that you can get the best rates.

ATMs can be found in major parts of the city such as airports, hotels, shopping centers and in main banks. It is available 24/7. However, there may not be ATMs available in remote areas of the city. You can also use international cards but it may not be acceptable in all of the ATM machines available.

Credit cards such as Visa, MasterCard and American Express are accepted in various hotels, restaurants, car rentals and shops. However, it may not come in handy if you are staying in a remote area such as villages and small towns, or areas that are away from tourist spots. It's better to bring cash than rely on your credit or debit card to be sure.

Electricity and Voltage

Rome's standard electrical voltage is 230 volts AC (50 cycles). Majority of the plugs and electric outlets have dual round pronged plugs. You may need a transformer or converter to aid your electrical equipment or appliances. It is highly recommended that you buy adaptors at various convenience and electrical/gadget stores in your own country so you can easily specify the equipment you need. You may need to use a power converter for European appliances that requires 110 Volts.

Public Holidays

Rome is the center of Catholicism in Europe, which means that they observe lots of different religious holidays aside from public holidays. Take note of the following dates and events so you can plan your trip accordingly.

- **New Year** (1 January)
- **Epiphany** (6 January)
- **Maundy Thursday** (date varies)
- **Easter Monday (**First Monday after Easter)
- **Liberation Day** (25 April)
- **Labour Day** (1 May)
- **Republic Day** (2 June)
- **Ferragosto or the Assumption of Mary** (15 August)
- **All Saints' Day** (1 November)
- **Feast of the Immaculate Conception** (8 December)
- **Christmas Day** (25 December)
- **Giorno di Santo Stefano** (26 December)

Health and Safety

You don't necessarily need vaccination certificates or other medical certificates upon entering Italy, although it's better to check if your airline requires it. If you happen to bring to your pets, you need to show its health or medical clearances to ensure that they have been vaccinated and free of rabies. You need to check with your airlines if they will allow it on – board. Please also check the consular website regarding the breed or the type of animal you can bring to Italy.

- **Potable Water**

The municipal water in Rome is approved by the World Health Organization and therefore safe to drink. It is free for locals and tourists. Mineral waters, including imported brands, can be found in stores and restaurants as well as airports or transportation terminals. There are several public water fountains in many landmarks.

- **Hospitals**

Hospitals in Rome are always available in case of any emergencies or accidents. Both public and private hospitals offer the highest quality of medical care and hospital facilities. The medical fee for attendance depends on the hospital and the procedure that will be done; patients will always be treated even if they cannot pay immediately, although the regulations may vary. Most medical professionals in public and private sectors can speak in English and Italian.

- **Smoking restrictions**

Smoking is banned in Rome's public areas or closed spaces, such as trains, airplanes, buses, restaurants, bars, hospitals, concert halls, museums, and theaters. There will be a penalty for those who will not observe the law. There is a designated floor in various hotels where you can smoke. Obviously, you are not allowed to smoke in air-conditioned areas or facilities.

Safety Tips

- Do not leave your valuables unattended. Your money, passport or travel documents should be in a safe place, or you should carry it with you at all times.

- Be vigilant and watch out for your valuables especially in crowded places.

- Beware of thieves, the most common threat in Rome is petty crimes such as pickpockets and tourist scams or scam artists.

- Beware of con artists who dressed up as police and pretend to check your papers. Often times, they will ask you for cash. Real police may check your documents but will never ask for any cash or your credit card.

- Observe the rules and regulations of public places especially inside shopping malls and tourist spots

For your peace of mind, Rome is frequently patrolled by police officers and they are very helpful, nonetheless, you still need to stay alert and mindful at all times. Crimes in Rome is almost non – existent, be vigilant anyway.

Public Hygiene and Environmental Regulations

Here are some rules you need to follow while wandering around Rome.

- Do not eat or drink in public transportations.
- If you are caught littering, drunk driving or urinating in public venues, you will be fined by authorities or get arrested.
- There aren't many public restrooms around Rome and they may not always be clean and sanitary. You will also need to pay a small fine to use a public restroom. Your best bet is to use the washroom of your hotel or inside the restaurants.

- Maintain cleanliness and clean as you go.

Customs

Upon arriving at the airport in Rome, you will need to be cleared by the department of customs or Immigration Officers. Here are the things you are allowed to bring to and from Italy:

Things You Can Bring to and from Italy:

International visitors can bring most personal Items including the following special items:

- fishing tackle
- a pair of skis
- two tennis racquets
- a baby carriage
- 400 cigarettes or a quantity of cigars or pipe tobacco not exceeding 500 grams (1.1 lb.)

If you are going to bring alcoholic beverages, you may need to check the limit via consulting the consular website. The are no limits on the amount of money you can bring, however, you must declare it (if it exceeds 12,500 €) to the Italian Customs office because it is proof that this is the same amount you have before entering the country, therefore you can also take out the same amount or less once you depart.

Travel Insurance

It is highly recommended that you acquire travel insurance before traveling to Rome. Inquire with your travel insurance company about the emergency coverage, contact numbers, and persons as well as the insurance policy. If you already have one, always carry with you the insurance policy and the insurance company hotline number for identification purposes in cases of emergencies.

Communication Services

Another central necessity that you need to have access to is the transmission lines and services. Obviously, when you get to another country, the mobile services, as well as internet services, will be different. Here are some things you need to keep in mind for you to be able to communicate effectively while you are in Rome.

- **Mobile Phones/Telephones**

You may rent a cell phone while you are in the city to make local or international calls easily. You may also opt to open your roaming services, although the charges will be a bit expensive (overseas charges) if you send international

SMS or calls. Telephone booths still exist in the city but you need to buy a telephone card for you to make calls.

- **Wi-Fi/ Internet Services**

The Wi-Fi and internet services in Rome are fast and accessible, although in some places such as remote areas or villages, access may be limited. Aside from staying connected, I'm sure everyone especially tourists can't fight the urge to update the social media world and their online status regarding their whereabouts while spending time in the Eternal City!

No worries, Rome got you covered. There are many hotspots around the city particularly in the primary public locations and tourist destinations such as department stores, gardens, centers, restaurants and dining places, hotels, transportation terminals, government buildings and public venues that are free! All you have to do is to open your Wi-Fi and connect to the Wi-Fi ID of a particular place so that you can have free internet access.

Internet cafes and hotels are also offering high – speed internet access but you may need to pay for it to rent the computers.

Emergency Numbers

You may need to keep these emergency numbers on your phone just in case any issues arise while you are in Rome:

- **General Emergency Number** – dial 112 on the telephone
- **National Police** – dial 113 on the telephone
- **Ambulance** – dial 118 on the telephone
- **Fire Department** – dial 115 on the telephone
- **Italian Red Cross** – call 06 5510
- **Central Police Station** – call 06 46861
- **City Police (Emergency)** – call 06 67691
- **Medical Assistance (Ambulance)** – call 118

Seasons in Rome

Rome, like most European cities, has 4 seasons; Spring is a mild and rainy season, summer starts from June to August, Autumn is quite humid and Winter in Rome is also mild. You will never run out of sunshine and a cool breeze in this city, which means it's perfect for tourists almost all year round.

In this section, you will learn what to expect in Rome's climate and weather so you can plan your trip accordingly.

Climate and Weather

As mentioned earlier, Rome has a Mediterranean sub – tropical climate. There could be frequent rain fall or showers around the month of November. The best time to tour the city or swim in the sea is between July and August because the air is quite warm and it has the most daily sunshine.

- **Spring:** between March and mid – April; has a relatively mild and rainy season. The last few weeks of April and the month of May have warmer days but the sea breeze keeps it cool.

- **Summer:** between June to August; July being the hottest month with an average temperature of 26°C (78°F). It can go up to 34 °C - 38 °C. The temperature in the Roman coast can be cooler than the city center.

- **Autumn:** usually between September to November. The temperature is mild and humid, with alternate periods of cloudy skies and occasional rains especially around the month of October. Frequent rains may begin in the last few weeks of November and the temperatures will also begin to drop for winter.

- **Winter:** between December to February. The coldest is January; the temperature can easily drop to 8°C (46°F) or even at 7.5 °C. December is the wettest month in Rome; the city usually experiences an average of 96 mm of rain.

Reminders:

- Always bring a bottled water to avoid dehydration during summer.
- Always bring an umbrella and jacket especially during winter or rainy seasons.
- Don't stay too long under the sun and always as much as possible stay in air – conditioned places if you can't tolerate too much heat.
- Avoid going to Rome around winter because it'll be harder to reach your destinations. You may want to schedule your trip around summer and autumn seasons.

Chapter Three: Getting In and Around Rome

After learning the different requirements you need before traveling to the Eternal City, the next thing you should know is how to navigate around it. Rome is home to the most brilliant city structure in the world. Its streets are perfectly set up for explorers and curious minds. If you have enough knowledge regarding Rome's port of entry and transportation services, you will quickly get to your destination with ease. So don't waste your time, energy and money, they are precious, and they should only be consumed by "City of God."

Learning how to navigate Rome is the key so that you can have an amazing experience visiting the site of the Roman Empire. In this chapter, you will learn the major transportation systems and port of entries including communication services to help you reach and explore different tourist destinations as well as far-flung places. So grab your map, your smartphone and set out to the first metropolis ever built by mankind!

Traveling to Rome by Plane

This obviously the easiest way to get to the city, you can ride Rome's national airline called Tarom as well as other major international airlines. Almost all airlines offer non – stop flights from Western cities and Central Europe to Rome's capital in Bucharest. International airlines such as Delta, KLM Alitalia, and Air France can also take you to straight to Bucharest.

Other flights to key towns in Rome are also being offered non – stop including flights to Arad, Bacau, Cluj, Constanta, Craiova, Oradea, Sibiu, Targu Mures and Timisoara. You can also ride to other European destinations through different European airlines including Blue Air, LOT, RyanAir, Wizz Air, Turkish Airlines, Austrian Airline, Lufthansa, and Tarom.

Traveling to Rome by Train

If you are in a nearby city or in any European countries, you can get to Rome via train. It will take around 4 hours or longer depending on which country or city you'll be coming from.

If you are coming from Budapest and you wish to go to one of Rome's key towns like Arad or Oradea, the travel time is approximately 30 hours or around 1 ½ day. The trip from Paris to Bucharest also lasts for more than a day.

Most train ticket allows several stopovers, so if you are travelling to other European cities, it can be a better and more affordable option to explore the continent. First and second – class sleepers are available for overnight trips.

For more info regarding the schedule of international trains to and from Romania, please visit <www.bahn.de> or <www.interrail.eu>

The fares may also vary depending on your chosen destination, please visit the websites above to get more info about the pricing and the available trips.

Traveling around Rome by Buses

You can explore different places and towns in Rome through riding a bus. This can be a better option because it is cheaper compared to taxis.

There are several bus companies that will take you to Romania's main districts. The Inter – City bus stations are located near train stations. If you want to know the pricing and bus schedules for domestic routes you can visit their website <www.autogari.ro)

Traveling around Rome by Car

If you want to have the luxury of exploring the city at your own pace renting a car might be the best way for you. You can discover Rome's hidden facets and go to remote areas not reachable by buses and too expensive for taxis. With today's technology, you can be sure to reach any destination you may want to visit. Make sure that the car has GPS. Having a Waze App or Google Map can always come in handy. If ever you do get lost, you can always ask for directions, the locals can understand and speak English most of the time, and they'll be happy to help.

Most rental car companies are located in airports and they also have offices in major cities. You can ask your hotel if they also offer a transportation service or if the travelling package you have has one. Rental policies vary from one company to another, so make sure you read their terms and conditions before signing up. The renters should be over 21 years old, must have a valid driver's license and a credit card.

Traveling around Rome by Train

Rome today followed the footsteps of its predecessors by building a railway network that connects and covers the whole city. Romans love to travel through trains, so if you wanted to talk Romans or Romanians and discover their way of life, then hop on board for a great adventure and travel like a local!

The domestic trains are safe and on time, however it doesn't run very fast compared to international trains, so if you are running late for some reason, it may not be the best option. However, if you are a tourist you can surely savor Rome's great scenery and relax while waiting for your destination.

There are different kinds of domestic trains in Rome:

- **Regional (R)** – this is the local train and it is also the cheapest but the slowest line.

- **Inter - Regional Trains (IR)** - it is much faster and a bit more expensive than regional trains, it can connect you to other towns from the main station.

- **Inter - City Trains (IC)** – It is the fastest and most expensive railway line in Rome.

The Inter Regional and Inter - City Trains require a seat reservation and a ticket. They also have sleeping and dining options (first or second – class) for overnight travellers.

If you want to purchase train tickets for domestic routes within Rome you can go at the train station ticket offices, rail ticket vending machines, and other authorize agencies. You can also purchase on board from the train conductor, however surcharge may apply.

If you want to check the train schedules please visit the following websites so you can plan your trip accordingly:

- www.cfrcalatori.ro
- www.InterRail.eu
- www.Bahn.eu

Traveling around Rome by Taxis and Uber

Taxis or cabs can come in handy if you are going to a place that may not be reachable by bus or are too far away from train stations or main areas. Most of them are always available in the pick-up area of the airport. These taxis can also be hailed in every city and major towns or contacted by phone for service. They are all metered, air-conditioned, and clean but can be quite expensive. The surcharges highly depends on when, where and what cab company you are on board. It might be wise to call the taxi companies for you to confirm the rates and average cost of the ride. According to most locals, if the driver asks for an extra charge just ignore them and get off the taxi. This may be impolite but it may come in handy. However, if the charge is reasonable, it's better to just pay for it to avoid getting into trouble.

For longer or extended trips you may need to negotiate with the driver. Authorized taxis should have a TAXI sign on the roof.

Using the Uber App is another easy way if you want to get to your destination without the hassle of figuring out the bus stations or train stations. The charges will depend on the distance and the driver can be contacted through the Uber app.

Fares for Taxi:

- Upon Entry: $ 0.5 - $ 1.2
- Trips within city limits: $ 0.8 - $ 2 / mile
- Trips outside city limits: $ 1.2 - $ 2 / mile
- Slow traffic or waiting time: $ 0.1 - $ 0.3 / minute

Fares for Uber: depends on the distance, and the type of car.

Chapter Four: Hotels and Accommodations

After learning about the ports of entry in Rome and the different ways on how you can get around this very historical city, the next thing you should know after arriving at the airport is where to stay. There are tons of options online and a lot of feedback from friends, and family who have stayed in the city - not to mention the thousands of social reviews and comments on different social networking sites.

The million dollar question is - where should you stay and how in the world are you going to choose the best accommodation in this great country?

In this chapter you will be provided with the list of what we consider to be the top 10 best hotel and accommodation districts in Rome. Some are very expensive, while others are a bit more cost-friendly.

You will also be given an overview of what to expect in a particular district, and the landmarks or attractions near the area. You can also choose according to your interests, so you can see what district may best fit your personality.

If you want to know the best fit for you in every aspect – financial, proximity, ambiance and overall experience, check out the following recommended hotel areas or accommodation district on the next pages.

1. *The Centro - Storico*

The *Centro Storico* or historic center is probably the best district for any tourist to stay in for the duration of their Roman holiday.

In this area you can find a labyrinth of medieval – like streets, cramped alleys with a touch of Renaissance Palazzi, lots of Baroque churches and of course the good ol' Italian pizzas! This district is where you can find many of Rome's biggest landmarks such as the Pantheon and the famous Piazza Navona. Pretty much everything you need to see is within walking distance.

The only downside is that the hotels and accommodations here are expensive since it is within the main city. You can however try searching for an Airbnb or search for cheap hostels to suit your budget. If you use Airbnb you can definitely stay in a quite historic place for a few days without breaking the bank. Prices are much cheaper during out of season months.

This district is highly recommended for romantic getaways, lovers, and couples out there. This is the most romantic spot in town. This is also the place where you can find literally every site that you need to see in Rome. It is also near Vatican City.

Here's a quick overview of the famous hotels around Centro - Storico:

- Navona Loft
- Hotel Raphael
- Hotel Impero
- Hotel Quirinale
- UNA Hotel Roma
- Gioberti Art Hotel
- Rome Sweet Rome
- Dimora Frattina
- La Dolce Vita Barberini
- Albergo Cesari

2. *Tridente*

Tridente is located in the northern section of Rome, it is known as Tridente mainly because it consists of three roads. This is the shopping district of Rome. You can find several designer boutiques in this part of town such as the famous Piazza del Popolo as well as many expensive restaurants and chichi bars. Piazza di Spagna (Spanish Steps) is the center of the area and it was once a stop on the Grand Tour in Rome; you can also meet and have a chat with locals.

Hotels and accommodations here are small but ultra – luxurious to meet the demands of international customers. Most hotels have fancy entertainment systems inside the room and also serve expensive Italian and International cuisines.

This district is best suited for shoppers and fashion lovers out there. There are lots of European brands, classy Romanian boutiques, fancy malls, and luxurious department stores. Tridante is also home to various entertainment venues, and it has a great nightlife as well. Be sure to bring lots of money if you plan to shop and buy stuff in this part of town. No cheapskate allowed!

Here's a quick overview of the famous hotels around the Tridente:

- Portrait Roma
- Hotel Panda
- Crossing Condotti
- Hotel Modigliani
- Hotel Forte
- Deko Rome
- Hotel Locamo
- Hotel Scalinata di Spagna
- La Piccola Maison
- Hotel Mozart

3. *Via Veneto and Villa Borghese*

If money is not a problem then this district is best suited for you. This is a 5 – star hotel district and the kind of people who usually come and stay here are the rich and famous. You will be pampered with its streets full of grand hotels, marble floors, uniformed doormen and luxurious spas. In this district you will treated like an emperor!

Via Veneto was once the heart of Dolce Vita – era Rome where fashionistas and superstars hangout. It's also full of history and quite near the city centre.

The only downside is that the restaurants are packed with tourists; you might want to check out a place near Via Veneto called Villa Borghese. You can have a fine dining here without too much tourists around.

You can also choose to stay in Villa Borghese because there are also lots of luxurious hotels around the area. The transportation is also very accessible, and quite close to the city center but relatively far enough to tourist hotspots.

Here's a quick overview of the famous hotels around the Via Veneto and Villa Borghese:

- Daphne
- Splendide Royale
- Ambasciatori Palace
- Hotel Majestic
- Grand Hotel Palace
- Hotel Ludovisi Palace
- Hotel Eden
- Sina Bernini Bristol
- Roma Vittorio Veneto
- The Westin Excelsior

4. Monti and the Celian Hill

If you wanted to stay in a place where you could feel like you are a red – blooded ancient Roman, then this is the perfect district for you. Historically, Monti is the red light district of ancient Rome, but today it is now an area filled with cool bars, delicious cuisines, and boutiques. The Colosseum is just walking distance from this part of town. It is also near the Celian Hill in the southeastern area wherein you can find low – key local restaurants, and a perfect place to talk to a bunch of Romans.

The district has a village vibe, and the hotels around are also filled with local stories. If you are on a budget there are lots of inexpensive accommodations around the area. There are also expensive hotels around.

It's highly recommended that you scout and roam around Monti and the Celian Hill for you to feel the vibe of what's it like to become a true – blooded Roman during the era of the Roman Empire. Even if there are a lot of tourists and the place is now transformed to a busy metropolis, the structures of the buildings around are still intact, the streets are still cramped and the atmosphere still echoes the glorious days of Rome. Aside from The Colosseum it is also near the Imperial For a, the Markets of Trajan and the Capitoline Hill.

Here's a quick overview of the famous hotels around the Monti and Celian Hill:

- Hotel Rosetta
- Palazzo Manfredi
- Hotel Colosseum
- Monti Palace Hotel
- Nerva Boutique Hotel
- Hotel Cristoforo Colombo

- Hotel Osimar
- Princeps Boutique Hotel
- Hotel Duca d'Alba
- Mercure Roma Centro Colosseo

5. *Testaccio and the Aventine Hill*

If you are a history buff or perhaps a scholar, then you are better off staying somewhere else! The Testaccio and the Aventine Hill are reserved for people who wanted to indulge in Roman gastronomy! This place is not just home to many authentic Italian and Roman cuisine; it's also the central produce market in all of Rome. If you wanted to eat and also check out how Romanians do their day to day "food shopping" then this is the place to be.

Testaccio was formed around an old slaughterhouse, but today it is home to authentic Trattorias, one of Rome's famous dishes. It is also known for being an unpretentious district among locals and also an off – beaten paths for tourists. You might also want to check out the tranquil Aventine Hill that is quite near in Testaccio. It is one of Rome's residential places and offers a place of exclusivity from all the hustle and bustle of tourists. There are quite a few hotels and restaurants around but the place is peaceful and also walking distance to various ancient Roman landmarks.

Here's a quick overview of the famous hotels around Testaccio and the Aventine Hill:

- Seven Suites
- Hotel Sant'Anselmo
- Hotel Villa San Pio
- Hotel Pyramid
- Cleopatra
- Abitart Hotel

- Il Gladiatore
- Bed & Breakfast Testaccio
- Hotel Domus Aventina
- A Casa a Testaccio

6. *Trastevere*

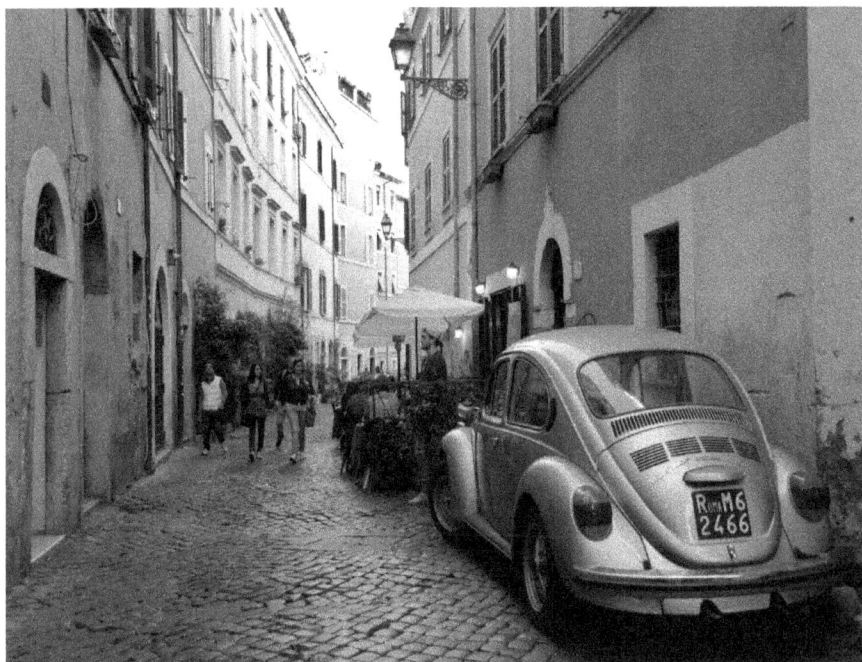

Trastevere is a great place if you are fond of taking photos because the street is filled with ivy – draped buildings, small parlor Italian pizzas, and the classic Roman roads. It was once a working class quarter but today it is one of the hotspots for tourists. Even if the narrow streets are now filled with cool bars and awesome restaurants, there are still lots of quiet places around the area where you can stay particularly in the eastern side of the district. Trastevere is located near the river, the Vatican and Centro – Storico are within walking distance.

The nightlife here is also fantastic for locals and tourists alike. This place is best suited for people who like to witness and experience the nightlife in Rome. It is also the center of Rome's artistic life.

Here's a quick overview of the famous hotels around the Trastevere:

- Hotel Trastevere
- Hotel Santa Maria
- Hotel Ripa Roma
- Roma Citta
- VOI Donna Camilla Savelli Hotel
- Residenza San Calisto
- Hotel San Francesco
- Borgo Papareschi
- Lungotevere Suite
- Luxury Trastevere

7. *Prati*

Prati is located in the northern part of Vatican City, but unlike other districts in Vatican, this is probably the "coolest" because it has wide boulevards, as well as numerous European restaurants and cocktail bars. Prati also has lots of inexpensive hotels that are best suited for pilgrims and backpackers.

The best thing about this area is that it is quite a peaceful place despite its buzzing streets.

You can indulge in Roman gastronomy, spend a fantastic night with locals, and also enjoy the solemnity of the place.

The only downside about this place is that it is far from the city centre, and even the central area of Vatican City itself. There aren't much interesting places or historical sites around the area but if you are in a budget, the hotels here can accommodate you so you can save your money for exploring the rest of Rome.

This area is also suited for sophisticated people who wanted to escape tourist's hotspots.

Here's a quick overview of the famous hotels around the Prati:

- Hearth Hotel
- Hotel Farnese
- Hotel Metropolis
- Hotel Gerber
- Rovati Guest House
- Casa 901
- Residenza Rioni Guesthouse
- Rienzo Apartment

- Domus Quiritum
- The B Place Hotel

8. *Ostia*

Ostia is a Roman district that is located near several beach resorts, and has a fantastic view of the sea. It is an outskirt part of Rome which means that it's very far from the city centre and most of Rome's tourist spots. However, if you wanted to stay and relax in the beaches of the Eternal City, this is the place best suited for you.

Lots of seafood restaurants and Romanian bars abound the area. You can do different activities here such as swimming, snorkeling or simply savor the tranquility of the resort. You may not find lots of tourists here since Rome is not a place known for its beaches; this is a great place for those who wanted to stay out of tourists spots.

Ostia is the home of Ancient Rome's harbor called Ostia Antica, if you choose to stay here, you will get to experience a sailor's atmosphere. Romans are not exactly known as sea navigators but they built great ships as part of their military. Experience waking up in the shores of the Roman Empire here in Ostia!

Here's a quick overview of the famous hotels around the Ostia:

- Ostia Antica Park Hotel
- Hotel Giulietta e Romeo
- Triangoli Residence
- Hotel La Scaletta
- Barceló Aran Blu
- Hotel La Riva
- Hotel Bellavista
- La Dolce Sosta
- B&B Soggiorno di Ostia
- Rifugio San Francesco

9. *Campo de' Fiori and the Ghetto*

This district is technically part of Centro – Storico but unlike the city centre, it's the part of town that is away from the hustle and bustle of tourists and locals alike. It has its fair share of historical sites such as the Pantheon, several cathedrals, and squares. The transportation is very accessible as well. It is also a perfect place for photo – ops, has lots of classy boutiques, and its street is also filled with famous restaurants such as Piazza Campo de' Fiori, café bars, wine bars and also trattorias.

The (Jewish) Ghetto is near Campo de' Fiori, you can also choose to stay here because the neighborhood has a great ancient – feel and the place also boasts of authentic Italian restaurants.

You can even rent an apartment in Ghetto's backstreets so that you can experience living like an ancient Roman for a couple of days. If you are a fan of the Renaissance period then this is the place best suited for you! You can find small to medium accommodations here that ranges from budget hotels to relatively expensive hotels.

Here's a quick overview of the famous hotels around the Campo de' Fiori and Ghetto:

- DOM Hotel
- Domus Ester
- Hotel Lunetta
- Hotel Sole Roma
- Casa de' Fiori Biscione
- Mama's Home Rome
- Town House Campo de' Fiori
- Residenza Navona First
- DAB Campo De Fiori
- Piazza Farnese Luxury Suites

10. *Vatican City*

The last but not the least is Vatican City. It is of course suited for tourists who are planning to do a pilgrimage trip in Rome. The endless religious structures, basilicas, cathedral and Vatican museums will surely excite any pilgrim and Catholics out there. The surrounding districts such as Borgo and Monte Mario offers various hotel accommodations, there are also lots of Italian and European restaurants around the area. Don't try to look for any hip bars or nightlife in this part of town because you will not find any, obviously. The only down side is if you stay in Vatican City, you could be bombarded with lots of tourists. Every year millions of pilgrims, locals and Europeans flock in this place especially if there are major events in the Catholic Church. You may want to book in advance to avoid running out of hotel near the area where you want to go.

Accommodations here can be quite pricey during special occasions; nevertheless if you are a true devotee, this is the perfect place to stay for the duration of your trip. Who knows you could see the Pope himself! Be connected with the divine, and be a part of the oldest and most influential religion in history.

Here's a quick overview of the famous hotels around the Vatican:

- Hotel Sant' Anna
- Gran Melia Rome
- Atlante Garden Hotel
- San Pietro La Corte
- Hotel della Conciliazione
- Starhotels Michelangelo
- Hotel Emmaus
- Hotel La Rovere
- Palazzo Cardinal Cesi
- Dei Consoli Hotel

Chapter Five: Dining in Rome

Once you have decided what district you're going to stay in for your trip, the next thing on the list is your eating destination! Rome is not only known for its historical districts but also for its savory dishes. In Rome, the local cuisine still holds a sacred place in the table; the city's dining culture is constantly evolving in a much slower pace compared to other major cities like New York or Paris. This is good news because even if the cuisines are constantly evolving, Rome's traditional and classy dishes are still preferred by many. The city is keeping up with the changing palates through incorporating new modern flavors with their traditional dishes.

In this chapter you will be given the top 10 cuisines that you need to try while you are in Rome, you will also be given a recommended list of restaurants that specializes in each cuisines to ensure that you won't miss out the greatest gastronomic places that Rome has to offer.

1. *Cucina Romana*

For those of you who wanted to try out dishes that had been passed on for centuries, then Cucina Romana is the kind of cuisine you should taste. It consists of several authentic and classic Romanian dishes combined with other European foods. Some restaurants also offer a blend of modern techniques with local flavors. The best part is that these dishes are very affordable. So if you are the kind of tourist who literally wanted to eat what the ancient Romans back then are eating then this kind of cuisine is for you!

Here are the best restaurants in Rome that specializes in Cucina Romana or Romanian cuisines:

- Armando al Pantheon
- Cesare al Casaletto
- Tavernaccia Da Bruno
- Roscioli
- Mazzo

2. *Pizza*

Perhaps the only regret we all have for Ancient Romans is that they haven't had the chance to experience and taste one of the greatest food that planet Earth has to offer – the Pizza. It is a true Italian signature dish, one that will continue to be eaten and celebrated for centuries. The authentic and original Italian Pizza is to die for if you decided to visit Rome or in Italy for that matter.

The Italian Pizza straight out of an Italian oven located in an Italian city that is cooked to perfection and served with passion by Italian chefs is probably one of the greatest and most sumptuous experiences you are ever going to have in Rome. This artisanal dish will surely keep your palate craving for more! The mozzarella is to die for!

Obviously, there are lots of pizza places and restaurants around Rome that offers every kind of pizza, they're all great but only a few made it to our highly recommended lists. Here's the list of the best pizza restaurants in Rome:

Neopolitan Style Pizza

- Tonda
- Sforno
- Sbanco
- La Gatta Mangiona

Thin Crust Pizza/ Sliced Pizza

- Da Remo
- Pizzeria Ostiense
- Pizzeria Emma
- Pizzarium
- Panificio Bonci
- Prelibato

Flavored Pizzas

- Antico Forno Roscioli
- Forno Campo de' Fiori

Pizzette

- Da Artenio

3. Fine Dining

The fine dining restaurants in Rome are not the best in the business so to speak, but if for some reason you need meet someone or you are on a romantic date, no matter how great the pizza is, it may not be the appropriate dish for your companion. If you are also craving for the finest European dishes or international cuisines you can find these restaurants in major malls and in the city centre. There is a unique mix of seafood dishes, pastas and Romanian cuisines.

Unfortunately there aren't a lot of great restaurants that has great ambiance or has an elegant atmosphere, your best bet in finding great fine dining restaurants is in luxury hotels or popular malls in the city.

Here some highly recommended restaurants that you might want to check out if you want to taste Rome's fine dining:

- Sanlorenzo
- Tempio di Iside

4. *Jewish Classics*

Rome is of course home to many Jews; the influence of Roman Jewish cuisines had stayed in the country for centuries. It has become a part of Romanian cuisine which is why you should give it a taste. Aside from meals, pizza, and pastas, there are several Jewish pastry shops that offer delicious and classic delicacies.

Here are the some Jewish restaurants that can be found in the city particularly around the Jewish Ghetto district:

- C'e' Pasta...e Pasta
- Boccione Forno del Ghetto
- Nonna Betta

5. *Street Food*

If you wanted to eat like a local or if you are in a hurry, you may want to just try Rome's various street foods. This includes fried pastries, sliced pizzas, and sandwiches. These are foods on the go; you may also want to try getting a street food if you wanted to hang out with some locals.

Testaccio and San Giovanni are home to many classic Roman sandwiches. Here are some places around the Rome that you need to check out if you want to try out their street food:

- Mordi e Vai
- Trapizzino
- Supplizio

6. Gelato and Pastries

This is the kind of food that is perfect for those who have a sweet tooth. The gelatos and pastries in Rome also tastes incredible and a favorite among tourists. You might want to also take home several pastries or gelatos so that you can enjoy it as a midnight snack or as a dessert after dinner.

Here are some gelato places and pastry shops that you should check out:

For Gelatos:

- Al Settimo Gelo
- Gelateria dei Gracchi
- Gelato di Claudio Torce'
- Fatamorgana
- Fior di Luna

For Pastries:

- Regoli
- Roscioli Caffe
- Andrea De Bellis

7. Coffee/ Café Bars

Coffee also abound in the city, so if you want to spend your morning or afternoon just savoring the entire city with a great aroma by your side, then you should check out the authentic Italian coffee shops around Rome. You can find lots of historic coffee shops that had been around for many years already, you can also find many new places where youngsters usually hang out, and there are also lots of café bars that uses third wave coffee techniques. Here are the some coffee shops around Rome that you need to check out:

- Sciascia
- Roscioli Caffè
- Pergamino
- Marjani Coffee

8. Wine and Cocktails

As mentioned in previous chapters, one of ancient Rome's contributions is wine production. They were the first civilization who learned how to create a wine and pretty much paved the way to the kind of wines we have today. Wines had been very symbolic in almost any civilization particularly in the religious sector. As a major example, the Catholic Church uses wine to represent the blood of Jesus Christ during the Eucharistic celebration.

Rome still offers the best wine today with an addition of the modern day cocktails and of course beer. Any meal especially during occasions will not be complete without these drinks.

Here are some of the best bars and restaurants in town that offer the best wines, cocktails and beers around Rome:

- Litro
- Goccetto
- Remigio
- La Barrique
- Ma Che Siete Venuti a Fà
- Open Baladin
- The Jerry Thomas Project
- Caffe Propaganda
- La Punta
- Whisky & Co
- Jerry Thomas Emporium
- Domus Birrae
- Bir e Fud Beershop
- Costantini

9. Cheeses and Meats

If you happen to like cheese and cured meats then Rome is the perfect place to buy some! Cheeses and cured meats (*Salumi and Formaggi*) are almost always part of every Romanian banquet or meal. You might want to check out and buy different types of cheese or purchase some cured meats so you can also do a DIY cooking at home.

Here are some places where you can find the best Italian cheese and cured meats in town:

- DOL
- Secondo Tradizione

- Roscioli
- Beppe e I Suoi Formaggi
- La Tradizione

10. European Cuisines

If you already had enough Romanian diet and want to take a break from it, you could try other European restaurants in Rome that also offers great international cuisines. Some of these restaurants still have a touch of Italian and Roman flavors, while some offers pure Mediterranean style dishes or a bit of both. There are also Japanese restaurants that offer veggies and seafood dishes.

Here are the top restaurants that can be found in Rome that somewhat offers non – Romanian dishes:

- Mesob
- Doozo
- Janta Fast Food
- La Torricella
- Tram Tram

Chapter Six: Tourist Spots in Rome

This is the chapter you've all been waiting for! Now that you have a basic idea about Rome, its people and its culture, and now that you are fully equipped with the travelling essentials you may need before you go to this sacred city, it's time to see the colossal places that it has to offer!

As mentioned before, you will never run out of things to see and do in Rome. Like any other European countries, the Eternal City is filled with history, tradition and a full cultural experience. Be mesmerized and let your jaw dropped (because this is the perfect city to let that happen) as you stand in awe before these magnanimous sites and ancient places that stood the test of time. It has something for everybody – the history buffs, the old soul, the young – at – hearts, the adventure seeker, and the pilgrims as well as for families and tourists looking for an amazing travel experience.

In this chapter, we will give you ten of the greatest and grandest places that the city of Rome has to offer. These places are the "Editor's Choice" in many publications and media organizations. These places are also the hottest spots for tourists around the world; prepare your body, mind and soul for a one – of – a – kind experience that you will always remember.

Get ready because the anciently known Capital of the World (*Roma Caput Mundi*) will let you know why and how it became the greatest civilization the world has ever seen.

1. *Roman Forum (Foro Romano)*

First stop is the famous Foro Romano! According to some locals and tourists, The Roman Forum is actually more interesting than the Colosseum, maybe because this is where you can find Ancient Rome's most important structures such as shrines, government houses and different monuments – which in itself is a tourist destination already. This is where all the action is at the height of the Roman Empire and back when it was still a Republican system. It served as the center of political, religious and civic life. It is the very heart of the greatest empire in the world.

If for some reason you wanted to go back in time and seize the city for yourself (why would you do that?) then you better go to the city's headquarters located at the Roman Forum!

The place was built around the 7th century B.C. and since then it had witnessed a lot of construction, destruction, re-construction and demolition - big and small over the years. Fortunately some of its famous structures survived such as the Curia Julia (site of the Roman senate), the Temple of Antoninus and Faustina, the Temple of Saturn, the Arch of Titus, the Arch of Septimius Severus, Atrium Vestae, Temple of Ceasar, the Regia (where the first Roman kings lived), the Temple of Concord and Basilica of Maxentius to name a few.

Unfortunately some of its other important structures had now become a shadow of its past glories symbolizing the end of an era from a by-gone age. Nevertheless, the ancient Roman atmosphere in this area is still very evident.

After you visit the Colosseum, this should be next to your list since the proximity is just very near. Your trip to Rome is not fully realized if you hadn't gone to the Roman Forum. Keep in mind that this is the center of everything – the powerhouse that brought the city to its all – time glory.

Directions:

The Roman Forum is off the Via dei Fori Imperiali. Metro stop: Colosseo (line B).

Ticket Prices and Schedule of Opening:

The Roman Forum is always open to the public.

2. *Ostia Antica*

Ostia Antica is one of the best historical Ancient Roman sites that is still intact today. It is where some of the ruins of the ancient city can be found particularly the port area because it is the closest to the sea. The Ostia Antica served as the gateway to the Roman Empire.

This place goes back to around 4th century B.C., and it is Rome's main port for hundreds of years. This is the place that witnessed the rise and fall of the ancient empire. Around 68 B.C. it was constantly attacked by pirates, which led to the seizing of the city by Pompey the Great that eventually caused damaged to the empire's Republican System.

Today, tourists can see many of the ruins of this ancient town including a preserved Roman theatre, military camp remains, the Baths of Neptune, several temples dedicated to ancient deities, and the Ostia Synagogue – believed to be one of the oldest known synagogues in all of Europe.

The best thing about this place is that there are many notable pieces of history tucked inside it. This site contains almost all the equipments used by the ancient locals that probably one way or another influenced the way we live.

You can visit several former Roman dwellings wherein you can see the shops, warehouses, public restrooms as well as ancient flats. This is pretty much the place to see if you wanted to know and feel what it's actually like to be a Roman back in the day.

Another great thing about it is that it's not actually crowded with tourists, mainly because it is located in the outskirts of the city, so you can take lots of photographs, walk around peacefully, and contemplate the rich history of the place without getting distracted by other tourists.

You can also visit a small museum in Ostia Antica that has lots of ancient artifacts. This place is also a venue for some events and concerts at certain time of the year.

Directions:

By Train: Take the Metro to Piramide station (line B). From there take the Roma-Lido line to Ostia Antica station. The site is right next to the station, just walk over the small bridge to enter Ostia Antica.

Ticket Prices and Schedule of Opening:

Adults €6.50

Children €3.25

Opening Times: 8.30am to 4pm (with late closing in the summer months)

3. The Pantheon

The Pantheon is undoubtedly one of the most preserved structures not just in Rome or in Europe but in the whole world! It was originally built in 25 B.C. by Marcus Agrippa, but the structure was destroyed in 80 A.D. because of the great fire in Rome. It was later re – constructed and completed during Emperor Hadrian's reign around 125 A.D. which is the same Pantheon that still exists today. Around 609 A.D. the Pantheon was converted to a Church which helped preserved it from destructions during wartime. This is also the place where Italian Kings and notable figures in politics and government were buried during the Renaissance period.

Today, the Pantheon is one of the most visited historical sites in Rome; the architecture and overall design of the building is probably the reason why it is beloved by many. Its domed roof that has an oculus opening at its peak is regarded as an architectural feat back in the day. The cast concrete that makes up this monumental structure is a testament of Roman's expertise when it comes to engineering, architecture and construction.

The Pantheon's roof is the largest dome in the world until the 15th century. You must visit this place, check out its amazing structure and savor its rich history. You are now seeing precisely what many local ancient Romanians had seen during their time. It is truly a great way to connect back to the people who started it all.

Directions:

The closest Metro station to the Pantheon is Barberini (line A) or Colosseo (line B) but the Pantheon is still at least a mile from both. Local buses or hop-on, hop-off tourist busses can take you from the metro stations to the Pantheon.

Ticket Prices and Schedule of Opening:

Entrance to the Pantheon is free! Make the most out of it!

4. Palatine Hill (Palatino)

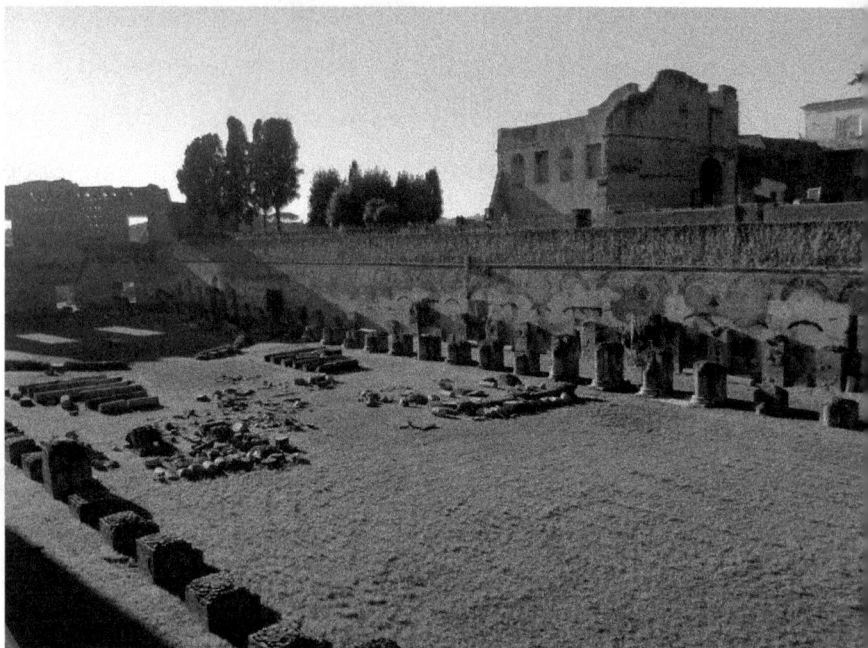

The iconic Palatine Hill is believed the place where Rome was born. If you are a major history buff, this is the best site for you. The Palatine Hill is one of Rome's Seven Hills and it houses most ancient sites both above the ground and the city under it.

According to legends, Romulus and Remus were raised and taken by a she – wolf at the Palatine Hill where they founded the city that would become Rome.

Romulus eventually killed his brother Remus to settle the dispute of who is the rightful leader of the new settlement, which is why the city is named after him.

During the time of the Republic, the Palatine Hill is a place for affluent Romans; it was already a coveted place around 1st century B.C., the location also became the home of Rome's most prominent figures including its first Emperor, Augustus who was born in 63 B.C.

Today the Palestine Hill is still comprised with some of Rome's greatest and must – see historical landmarks including the House of Augustus, the House of Livia (the emperor's wife), as well as other homes of Roman emperors.

If you wanted to experience living like a true ruler and king, this is the place to go to. The birthplace of everything before Rome became the city it was today.

Directions:

The Palatine Hill is located in Rome and can be reached by buses 60, 75, 85, 87, 117, 271, 571, C3 and 850. Tram 3 stops nearby and its entrance is a 5 min. walk from Circo Massimo metro station on line B.

Ticket Prices and Schedule of Opening:

A combined ticket to the Palatine with the Colloseum and Forum costs €12, €7.50 reduced. It is advisable to check the official website before visiting.

The Palatine Hill is open daily 8:30am - one hour before sunset. Palatine museum open 9am-6pm. Ticket office shuts one hour before closing.

5. *Trevi Fountain (Fontana di Trevi)*

The Trevi Fountain is another tourist hotspot in Rome. It was designed by Nicola Salvi and was continued and completed by Giuseppe Pannini around 1762.

It is one of the most iconic fountains and landmark in the 18th century. The fountain depicts several ancient deities that are regarded as gods and goddesses; legend has it that if you throw one or two coins in the fountain using your right hand over your left shoulder, you will fall in love with a Roman, and also marry that same Roman – which I personally think is just something that the single Romans looking for love back in the day, randomly invented to give themselves hope or to make people believe in myths and legends. Nevertheless, you should try it for legend's sake, and experience this great long – time tradition, you got nothing to lose! Tourists also throw their coins into the fountain's water to assure their return to the Eternal City.

The Fountain of Trevi is also a great example of a baroque design because of its mythological characters. Neptune, the Roman god of the sea, is designed to look like it is emerging from the waters, surrounded by Tritons. The landmark underwent extensive restorations and was reopened in November 2015. It is best to go here at night because the lights illuminate the fountain, which is also perfect for photo – ops.

Directions:

Nearest metro to the Trevi Fountain: Barberini (Line A)

Ticket Prices and Schedule of Opening:

The Trevi Fountain is viewable at all times.

6. *The Spanish Steps* (Scalinata della Trinità dei Monti)

The Spanish Steps is another famous attraction in Rome. It is a grand staircase with 138 steps that leads down to the famous Piazza di Spagna. It was designed by an Italian architect named, Francesco de Sanctis in 1726.

The Spanish Steps was named after the Spanish Embassy nearby. It was the most popular spot for tourists and locals alike especially during the 18th and 19th century.

Once you climbed up the Spanish Steps, you'll also be able to see the Keats – Shelly house, some beautiful Roman homes and it also lead to a Roman market. Some tourists and locals recommend staying here at night when it is not too crowded, you can also opt to have a snack in the coffee shops or grab a gelato while you mingle with tourists and Romanians.

There are a lot of Italian shops, restaurants and vendors around the area where you can buy delectable Romanian street food as well as some souvenirs after you spent some time gazing at the marvelous view from the top.

Another fun fact about the Spanish Steps is that this is the place where famous Roman writers Balzac and Byron hang out to get a dose of inspiration. Make sure to bring comfortable shoes and take lots of photos at the top overlooking the city of Rome.

Directions:

The nearest metro to the Spanish Steps is Spagna (line A).

Ticket Prices and Schedule of Opening:

The Spanish Steps is a public area.

7. Hadrian's Villa (Villa Adriana)

The Hadrian Villa is probably the best – preserved Roman village today. It was built around the 2nd century and became the powerhouse for Ancient Rome at the latter years of Emperor Hadrian's reign.

The complex covers 250 acres of land and comprises 30 buildings including a swimming pool, ancient libraries as well as Maritime Theater. Perhaps one of the least but intriguing discoveries in this villa is Emperor Hadrian's personal toilet, which was known to be the ruler's escape from the stress of his imperial life.

The best part is that not a lot of tourists visit here because it's a bit difficult to access, but it is famous spot among historians, scholars, archaeologists and academics.

Hadrian's Villa is a great tribute to one of Rome's greatest emperor, just be sure to wear comfortable shoes and bring lots of water especially during the summer because it will take you about 3 hours to tour the whole complex. Nevertheless, it's a great way to spend your day while you are in Rome.

Directions:

Tour companies offer convenient trips to Hadrian's Villa from Rome. If you travel yourself by car, take the A24 to the Tivoli exit (towards SP51) and follow signs to "villa adriana". Using public transport, take the Metro line B to Ponte Mammolo and from there takes the bus towards Via Prenestina.

Ticket Prices and Schedule of Opening:

€10 Adults; 9am-5pm Summer, 9am - 3pm Winter

8. Pyramid of Cestius

The country of Egypt for sure still houses the best pyramids in the world, but the city of Rome will not be called an Eternal City if it doesn't have a bit of everything that Europe and the Mediterranean has to offer.

The Pyramid of Cestius is a tomb built for Caius Cestius around 18 – 12 B.C. It is made out of marble and brick and it stands at about 35 meters. The architectural style of Egypt swept the city of Rome which is why you can also find Egyptian – inspired structures during the times of the Roman Empire.

You can find lots of frescoes that depict Roman mythology scenes; you can also still find inscriptions that give details about its dedication and construction. The pyramid is later set into the Aurelian Walls to ensure its preservation.

The Pyramid of Cestius is something that you should check out because it is very rare to find ancient pyramids these days, and because Rome is an unlikely place to find one, it will surely be a great experience.

Directions:

The Pyramid of Cestius is easily reached from Pyramide metro station on line B.

Ticket Prices and Schedule of Opening:

The Pyramid of Cestius is viewable at all times from the outside.

9. Ancient Appian Way (Via Appia Antica)

The "road" in the famous phrase "all roads lead to Rome" is probably because of the Via Appia Antica. It is the most important and oldest road in Rome during the time of the ancient empire. It is originally built in 312 B.C. and was extended around 191 B.C. It is over 550 km that reaches the southeast of the city or what they call the "heel" of Italy, making the Via Appia Antica a gateway to the east.

Julius Caesar became the curator of the Appian Way in 66 B.C in order for him to gain electoral votes. He restored and improved the ancient highway through borrowing huge sums of money, which in one way or another, gained him the votes he needed to become Rome's emperor. Little did he know that this road is going to be the predecessor of the way we built our highways and roads today.

Lots of historical events have occurred in Via Appia Antica including the execution of Spartacus' army, and it is the road where the Roman Military marched; legend has it that it was also the road where Christ appeared to Peter who was fleeing at the time, and convinced him to return to Rome after the execution.

It was also once a popular location for many Roman tombs and catacombs which is something that you can still see today scattered on the sides of the road including the Mausoleum of Cecilia Metella, Catacombs of San Callisto and St. Sebastian's Catacombs. You can also find other monuments like the Circus of Maxentius, Villa dei Quintili and the Baths of Caracalla.

Filled with many historical landmarks and remnants of the former empire, the Appian Way is surely a must – see for tourists. The road has so many significant stories you need to learn, and many incredible sights you need to see. Be sure to visit this place because every details of it will provide you a lot of insights from its glorious past. The long trek is definitely worth it, just make sure to wear comfy shoes and don't forget to bring your camera or smartphone!

Directions:

Located in southern Rome, you can find it outside Porta San Sebastiano; buses 118 (from San Giovanni) or 218 (outside the Piramides metro station) should get you there.

Ticket Prices and Schedule of Opening: Prices and opening times vary for each site along Via Appia Antica (many close an hour before sunset).

10. The Colosseum (Colosseo)

Ah! The structure that needs no introduction, regarded as one of the best and greatest wonders of the world, no other than the colossal and phenomenal Colosseum! You haven't gone to Rome if you haven't seen this ancient arena! Perhaps this place represents the sheer power and impact of the Roman Empire for many centuries to come. This is where gladiators collide, this is where bloodshed is constantly drawn, and this is the pride of the most powerful empire the world has ever seen.

Standing at about 48 meters with a circumference of 573 yards that can hold over 50,000 spectators, experts say that the Colosseum is without a doubt one of the most spectacular engineering and architectural feat in world history. It was built during the 1ˢᵗ century A.D. for the sole purpose of entertainment! So if you are wondering, yes! The concept of live events, arena gatherings, concerts, sports shows and theatrical venues started thousands of years ago because of the influence of ancient Romans.

The Colosseum was originally called the Flavian Amphitheatre, after Vespasian's family name. Vespasian is the man who helped the Roman Empire prevent downfall, but unfortunately he didn't get to see the arena's completion. The Colosseum is located and built inside the palace of Emperor Nero, particularly in his former garden to emphasize the point that the Vespasian family is different from the worst emperor of all time. It was built mainly for the people.

What's amazing is that, the structure was completed in just a short amount of time despite of its size and complexity. It was decorated with marble and stone that is symmetrical – a true magnificent piece of ancient architecture.

The Colosseum was opened by Titus, Vespasian's successor and son. He marked the opening with 100 hundred days of games. The arena remained Rome's amphitheater until the end of the Roman Empire. This is where gladiators fight to the death, and where people who are accused of crimes were put to the test.

The structure despite of its ancient roots are still pretty much intact after all these years, it just goes to show the strong foundation that built the Roman Empire from the ground up.

Today, many new places inside the Colosseum are open to the public such as the underground hallways where gladiators would prepare before their fight and ponder their mortality as well as higher areas of the arena wherein one can have a perfect view of the Roman Forum. You can find lots of artifacts inside the museum that is also located within the Colosseum.

Visiting this place will give you lots of insights about the kind of life that the ancient Romans lead back in the day - their cruel side perhaps - but interestingly it also paved the way for the next civilizations and probably made them realize that the "fighting to the death part" is probably not a good idea. Thank God that kind of tradition was not carried out by humanity to this day!

It is best to visit the Colosseum early in the morning, or late afternoon preferably with a tourist guide so that you can learn the most important things about Rome's pride.

Directions:

The Colloseum has a dedicated metro station, Colloseo, which is on line B.

Ticket Prices and Schedule of Opening:

Mid Feb-mid Mar: 9am-5pm; Mid-end Mar: 9am-5.30pm; Apr-Aug: 8.30am-7.15pm; Sept: 8.30am-7pm; Oct: 8.30am-6.30pm; End of Oct-mid-Mar: 8.30am-4.30pm. Tickets cost €12.

Chapter Seven: Churches in Rome

Rome is also the city that is now the capital of the Catholic faith. It is where the Pope, the highest leader of the Catholic Church, resides and spent most of his time governing and practicing one of the oldest religions in the world. For Catholics, Rome is the go – to place for everything sacred and holy.

You can find all the greatest, grandest and most ancient church structures and basilicas here in Rome particularly in the Vatican City.

It is home to many religious figures, ancient old relics and artifacts, and the very foundation of Catholicism itself.

In this chapter we will give you the top 10 churches, basilicas and religious structures in Rome that is fit for any Catholic devotee or any pilgrims even of other religions. Rome is home to the faith that the great Lord Jesus Christ Himself established 2,000 years ago, the faith that accepts any kind of faithful, and one of the biggest religions filled with rich history that stood the test of time. Prepare to marvel at the architecture and design of these Churches that is all created for the glory of God.

1. St. Peter's Basilica (Basilica di San Pietro in Vaticano)

First on the list is every Catholic's favorite – St. Peter's Basilica. This is perhaps the most popular church in both the ancient and modern world. The basilica is dedicated St. Peter, the first bishop of Rome and the first Pope of the Catholic Church. It was originally built under Emperor Constantine back in 326 A.D. Around 1452, it was completely re-constructed under Pope Nicholas V.

Once you enter this grand church, you will immediately see the famous sculpture of Michelangelo called Pieta. It was completed in 1500 and it is now encased in a glass panel. Other famous artifacts inside St. Peter's Basilica is the Chapel of the Sacrament, the great dome designed by Michelangelo, St. Peter Enthroned, the Papal Altar and tombs of the famous Popes created by famous Italian artist Bernini.

St. Peter's Basilica is where all the most important Catholic events are being held. This is the goal of every Christian pilgrim; to be able to see the great ancient old structure, be able to attend the Holy Eucharist presided by the Pope and of course be part of the one of the greatest religious gathering in Europe and in the world.

The church is located in Vatican City in the famous St. Peter's Square where millions of Catholics gather every year especially during the Lenten Season, and Christmas Eve. It is the place where Catholics from all over the world gather if there's a canonization of a saint or appointment of a new Pope.

2. St. John Lateran (San Giovanni in Laterano)

Before the Popes began officially residing in St. Peter's Basilica, the Basilica of St. John Lateran was the Papal residence at the time when the Popes returned from exile in Avignon. The church started its construction in 313 A.D. and it had undergone through many renovations around the 16th and 17th century.

Famous architect Alessandro Galilei designed the wide façade of the church in 1735 which became a masterpiece of the Baroque period. The door of the Curia is made out of bronze, and the apse is made out of fine mosaics where it houses copies of early Christian documents. You can also enter a 13th century masterpiece called the Cloister. It was designed by Vassalletti also a famous Roman architect. You can also see the oldest octagonal baptistery in Christian history and in all of Europe called San Giovanni in Fonte. It was built during Constantine's time.

Across the Pizza San Giovanni is the church of Scala Santa that contains a flight of 28 marble steps that is believed to be from Pontius Pilate's palace in Jerusalem brought by St. Helen (Constantine's mother) to Rome. Every year, Catholics climb these stairs on their knees to commemorate Christ's Passion. You will also see the Egyptian obelisk inside the Piazza San Giovanni which is one of the tallest monuments in Rome.

You can find the St. John Lateran Church in Piazza San Giovanni in Laterano.

3. Basilica di Santa Maria Maggiore

The Santa Maria Maggiore is one of the city's four patriarchal basilicas and also one of the most important pilgrimage churches that faithful's and tourists alike flock to. The church has a record of being the only church in Rome to celebrate the Holy Eucharist every single day since the 5th century.

According to catholic stories, the location of the church was determined by Pope Liberius back in the 4th century because he apparently received guidance from the Virgin Mary that a church should be built where the snow will fall the following day.

The snow then fell on the Esquiline hill on August 5, and so that is the place where the Pope ordered to build a church which is now one of the most renowned in the world. It contains Rome's tallest and one of the oldest campaniles until the 15th century; it is made out of gold coffered ceiling (the first gold from America) and it was created by the famous architect, Giuliano da Sangallo.

The church also contains Rome's oldest mosaic that goes back to the 4th century. It has one of the longest and most majestic aisles in Roman churches. If you visited the church early in the morning, you can surely see the intricate details of the 13th century mosaics that depict various Old and New Testament themes. The church's interior is also decorated with a geometric colored stone known as Cosmatesque work, which is considered one of the supreme achievements in Roman architecture.

The church is located in Piazza di Santa Maria Maggiore in Rome, it's also filled with tourists and pilgrims so be sure to arrive early.

4. St. Peter in Chains (San Pietro in Vincoli)

If you don't like the hustle and bustle of St. Peter's Basilica, then no worries, there is another church that also bears almost the same name. St. Peter in Chains was built in 431 and is one of the oldest churches in Rome. The most famous relic in the high altar is St. Peter's clothes which were believed to be worn when he was in Mamertine Prison. The church had undergone through alterations and renovations over the years. You can find twenty columns with Doric capitals and also the 15 century tomb of Cardinal Nicholas of Cusa along the north aisle.

Probably the most import piece of art aside from St. Peter's relic is Michelangelo's sculpture of Pope Julius II around the early 16th century which is located in the south transept of the church. It is located in Piazza di San Pietro un Vincoli.

5. Santa Maria sopra Minerva

The former temple of Minerva is now the largest Gothic church in the city. It was constructed around 1280 and was completed in 1453. It is run by the Dominican order and can easily be found because it is located in the city center. The church played an important role in the religious life of the city.

You can find the best funerary chapels inside the basilica called Carafa Chapel located at the south transept. The Carafa Chapel is also famously known as the Chapel of Annunciation of St. Thomas, it is known for its frescoes that were made by Filippo Lippu in 1489.

The high altar houses the relics of St. Catherine of Siena, and in front of the altar is Michelangelo's statue of the Risen Christ. However, during his time the statue was criticized for looking more like a pagan than Jesus Christ, but it was also admired by other sculpture artists later on. In fact according to painter, Sebastiano del Piombo, the details of Christ's knees in Michelangelo's artwork is worth more than all the building in Rome!

It is located in Piazza della Minerva in Rome, near the beloved marble elephant created by Bernini and also behind the famous Pantheon.

6. Santa Maria del Popolo

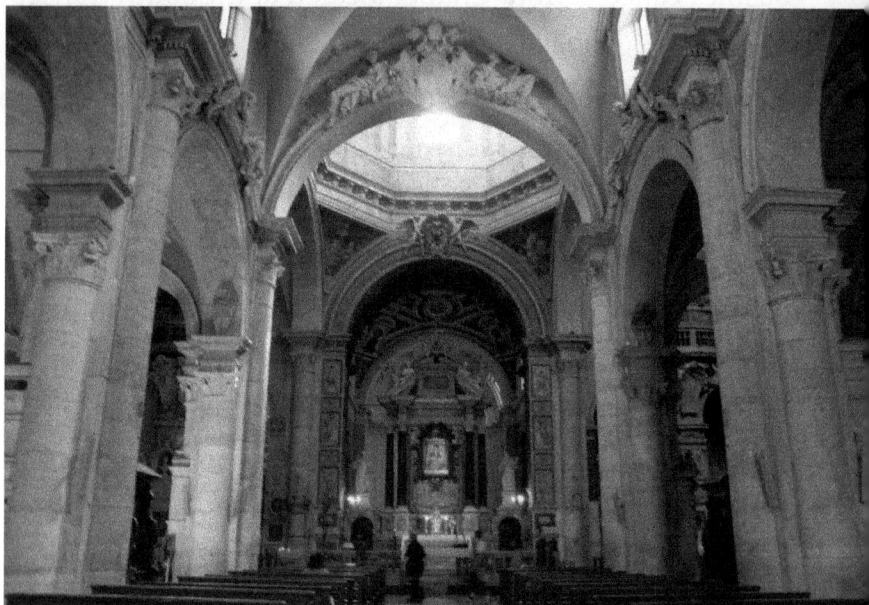

The Santa Maria del Popolo is probably the most intriguing church built in Rome because legend has it that it was built for the purpose of driving the evil spirits of Emperor Nero. The church's Renaissance façade, campanile and dome were all added by Bramante in 1505, and were later restored by Bernini. Another interesting fact is that this is where Martin Luther stayed during his visit to Rome because he was an Augustinian.

The three aisles and side chapels of the church contain tombs which were created by Andrea Sansovino.

You can also find frescoes that depict the Coronation of the Virgin Mary created by Pinturicchio. The side chapels was designed by Raphael in 1515, and the Cesari Chapel contains two pictures called the Conversion of St. Paul and the Crucifixion of St. Peter which was created by Caravaggio. You can find the church in Piazza del Popolo.

7. *San Clemente*

Built by early Christians before 385 A.D., San Clemente was the one of the oldest and most intricately detailed churches in Rome. It also contains the shrine of Mithras. A new basilica was rebuilt around the 12ᵗʰ century (which is now the church we see today), after it was destroyed by the Normans in 1084.

The upper part of the church reflects the old basilica, its nave is where the congregation worships, and the higher altar are for the clergy. The ancient pillars, marble floor, beautiful screens, the Easter candlestick as well as the tabernacle of the bishop's throne are all rich decorated with scenes from the Old and New Testament.

The frescoes created by Masolino from the Renaissance period are also present in the church's walls. There is also an excavated underground passage that leads to a Roman house from the 2nd century that contains the shrine of Mithras, one of the famous gods in Roman mythology. The church is located in Via San Giovanni in Laterano.

8. Santa Maria in Cosmedin

The Santa Maria in Cosmedin is located on the south side of the Piazza Bocca della Verita. The church is one of the best examples of medieval architecture of Ancient Rome. The construction started out in 772 and was completed in 1124. Interestingly, this architectural wonder has a two – story porch with a canopy and it also has a 7 – story campanile. The church's interior including the floor, screens, and bishop throne are all made up of marble that is created by the Roman Cosmati family.

The aisles of the church are painted with frescoes, and its columns' materials are remnants of ancient sites. You can also see a crypt where the early Christian tombs are buried. Although the church is well – built and was another architectural feat, it's not well – known for its interior neither its rich history. It is popular among tourists for its large stone mask called the Bocca della Verita or the Mouth of Truth. Tourists love to line up just to take photos of their hands inside the mouth of the stone mask. It was believed that this is where the ancient Romans swore oaths because the mouth was supposed to bite anyone who is lying.

9. *Santa Maria in Trastevere*

The Santa Maria is believed to be one of the first places in Rome where early Christians held their gatherings. The church was constructed around 221 and was finished in 340. It was then rebuilt during the Baroque period in 12th century.

The church contains a Romanesque campanile, a portico, and a mosaic decorated façade. You can also see a marbled floor as well as coffered wood ceiling and an apse made out of mosaics which you will surely gaze upon. It was regarded as a masterpiece of medieval art during the Renaissance period.

The mosaics were created by Pietro Cavallini in the late 13th century that depicts the lives of Christ and the Virgin Mary. The 15th century old tabernacle made by Mino del Reame can be found at the west end of the nave. It's definitely worth checking out. The church is located in Piazza Santa Maria in Trastevere.

10. Santa Sabina

The exterior and interior of Santa Sabina Church is created by Peter of Illyria in 425 – 432 B.C. The basilica was embellished around 824 but fortunately this early Christian church survived until this day.

The entrance of the Church is made up of one of Rome's oldest mosaic, and the porch is also one of the oldest wooden carved doors in Christian art that dates back from 432. The door depicts scenes form the Old and New Testament, fortunately 18 of the original 28 panels still exists today.

The interior of the basilica contains 20 Corinthian columns that are made out of Parian marble. The church is also adjoined with the Dominican monastery where St. Thomas Aquinas spent his time contemplating. It has a beautiful Romanesque cloister, and the best part is that tourists can also enjoy a great view of the Trastevere, Tiber sea, Vatican City and Piazza Venezia. The church is located in Piazza Pietro d'Iliria.

Chapter Eight: Museums in Rome

The Eternal City is also where the most ancient relics and artifacts can be found. Unlike any other European countries, Rome is where both civilization and faith was mainly established, so you can just imagine many pieces of the past being housed and preserve in this city for eternity. Both the history buffs and devotees or religious people will surely enjoy and quench their thirst for curiosity by going to many of the world's oldest museum here in Rome and just savor bits and pieces of how humanity came about.

1. Museum of the Ara Pacis

When Augustus stepped down as Rome's Emperor around 13 B.C., the Senate wanted to commission a monument of Rome's first emperor to mark his achievements of peacefully ruling the empire, which prompted them to build the Ara Pacis Augustae altar. It is just a simple center altar made up of marble walls that is carved gloriously to hail the former emperor as well as his family, and the peace and prosperity that he brought to the Roman Empire.

The altar was pieced together from different scattered fragments around the 20th centrury. Today, it is now housed in a modern shell created by Architect Richard Meier, an American. The Ara Pacis museum is also an exhibition venue. It is one of the oldest museums in Rome that honors their first ever ruler.

Location: Lungotevere in Augusta, 00186
Telephone Number: 00 39 06 0608
Website: www.arapacis.it

2. Borghese Gallery

One of the most preserved art collection in Rome is Titan's Sacred Profound Love as well as the sculpture of Apollo and Daphne created by Bernini is housed in Borghese Gallery. The Borghese Gallery is assembled by Cardinal Scipione Borghese in his garden villa around the 17th century. The gallery also houses the statue of Pauline Bonaparte.

Around the villa is a 17th century aviary and what they call as secret gardens. Most of the time the secret gardens are close but a company in Italy called Bell'Italia 88 sometimes runs tours.

If you want to visit this famed gallery, you should book ahead of time because there's a designated timeslots for visitors since it's always packed with tourists. You must be 30 minutes ahead of time before to pick up your gallery ticket.

Location: Piazzale del Museo Borghese 5, 00197
Telephone Number: 00 39 06 32810
Website: www.galleriaborghese.it

3. Capitoline Museums

Popes for over the last 250 years had been collecting different artworks which are now housed in Capitoline Museum. It is also one of Rome's oldest museums dating back around 1734. Several artworks are now in either the two palazzi of Piazza del Campidoglio which was designed by Michelangelo.

You can also find colossal statues in Palazzo dei Conservatori including Rome's emblem which is a she – wolf with suckling twins (Romulus and Remus) – perhaps one of the well – known bronze statues in Rome's museum. Other famous artworks include paintings by Titian, Tintoretto and Caravaggio. You can also check out Marcus

Aurelius' equestrian statue that dates back around the 2nd century as well as Pope Urban VIII statue created by Bernini. If you head to the Palazzon Nuovo you can find many ancient statuary collections.

The ticket costs around €2 because it includes access to the Centrale Montemartini which is also highly recommended – in fact that museum is included in this list!

Location: Piazza del Campidoglio 1, 00186
Telephone Number: 00 39 06 0608
Website: www.en.museicapitolini.org

4. Centrale Montemartini

The Centrale Montemartini is without a doubt one of the greatest museum for Rome's panoply of ancient offerings. The museum was a former power station that's why you'll see huge turbines, cogs and boilers around the venue, the best part is that they've polished it up so that it will look like a backdrop for particular artwork pieces coming from Capitoline Musuem.

The major centerpiece is a huge statue of goddess Fortuna with her dreamy muse called Polymnia. It is considered as a hybrid of an ancient artwork and also an architectural decoration. You can visit the museum's website for updates on kids' activities and the occasional jazz concert.

Location: Via Ostiense 106, 00154

Telephone Number: 00 39 06 0608

Website: www.en.centralemontemartini.org

5. *Doria Pamphilj Gallery*

The Doria Pamphilj Gallery, now headed by British siblings, comprises an art collection by Doria Pamphilj and her family who were aristocrats that dates back around 1760. The highlights included a portrait of Pamphili pontiff Innocent X created by Velázquez which also served as an inspiration for another artist – Francis Bacon in 1953 who created the "screaming pope."

You can also find other masterpieces by Caravaggio, Titian, Raphael, Bernini, Breughel the Elder and Hans Memling.

The ticket price includes an audio guide narrated by Prince Jonathan Pamphili himself! For a multi-sensoral experience, you can join the Saturday tour accompanied by an art historian and a live early music orchestra. Tickets may be quite expensive and booking may be needed.

Location: Via del Corso 305, 00186
Telephone Number: 00 39 06 679 7323
Website: www.dopart.it

6. *Maxxi Museum*

The Maxxi museum houses collections of contemporary architecture and 21st century arts museum; it's also the venue for various exhibits focusing on architectural themes. It is located in a hip district in northern Flaminio designed by Zaha Hadid, a Pritzker Prize – Winning architect. Locals love to come to this place because aside from the art collections, the space that surrounds it is also interesting. Crowds flock to the piazza while sipping a good cup of coffee on a sunny weekend. You can also check out

Neve di Latte – one of Rome's sought after ice – cream shops after you roam around the Maxxi Museum.

Location: Via Guido Reni 4a, 00196

Telephone Number: 00 39 06 320 1954

Website: www.fondazionemaxxi.it

7. *Museum and Crypt of the Capuchins*

What was once an eerie crypt was renovated and turned into a museum of monk experiences. The Crypt of the Capuchins Museum houses artifacts that belong to

Franciscan missionaries which were believed to be taken or confiscated from the natives of the particular place these priests or monks went to. You can also find rooms dedicated for the order's heroes and saints. There is also a 17th century painting of St. Francis made by Caravaggio.

The main attention – getter is of course the crypt itself; you can check out the bones of many Franciscan monks from by gone generation buried in soil that came from Jerusalem. It is arranged in an artistic way on the walls and ceilings as well as incorporated into a macabre chandelier. At the entrance, you will see a very cool and interesting message that reads: 'You will be what we now are'.

Location: Via Veneto 27, 00187
Telephone Number: 00 39 06 8880 3695
Website: www.cappucciniviaveneto.it

8. *Museo della Civiltà Romana*

The Museo della Civiltà Romana is located in the southern business district of Rome, and was erected at the time of Italy's Prime Minister Mussolini. It houses artifacts and pieces of history from the ancient sites of Centro – Storico. You can find carvings in Trajan columns as well as other 3rd century A.D. ancient site replica.

Tourists can also visit the nearby Palazzo dei Congressi – an iconic European structure that dates back in 1930 – which is just across the museum.

Location: Piazza G Agnelli 10, 00144

Telephone Number: 00 39 06 0608

Website: www.en.museociviltaromana.it

9. *Palazzo Altemps*

The Palazzo Altemps comprises of several artworks and ancient statues from four local dynasties. You see back then, rich and powerful Roman aristocrats and their families are fond of collecting classical statuary. Apparently, that's the craze back in the 16th and 17th century. So most of them will collect and even fix broken sculptures by hiring a sculptor of their own just to preserve such collections – perhaps they knew that it needed to be fixed because one day it's all going to be preserve in a museum and they will be remembered.

Well, it did! The collections from generations of Roman families are still intact today. You can see Ares' statue which was fixed by Bernini, as well as an Athena statue created by Alessandro Algardi.

The ticket includes entrance to Crypta Balbi, Palazzo Massimo and the Baths of Diocletian.

Location: Piazza di Sant'Apollinare 46, 00186
Telephone Number: 00 39 06 3996 7700
Website: www.archeoroma.beniculturali.it

10. Palazzo Massimo alle Terme

The Palazzo Massimo alle Terme is a 19th century palazzo that houses various collections of classical art. The building was formerly a Jesuit school.

You can find Roman and Greek sculptures such as Discus Thrower and Augustus as High Priest on the ground floor of the museum. You can also find a mummy from Grottarossa, in Rome's northern periphery. Ancient Romans were fascinated by Egyptian artifacts such as mummies, pyramids and obelisks although they didn't adapt embalming.

The Mummy of Grottarossa is located in the second floor where the ancient room's wall is decorated with bright colors. You can also check out the plant-and-bird-filled triclinium (dining room) from Livia's villa north of Rome. The ticket includes entrance to Crypta Balbi, Palazzo Altemps and the Baths of Diocletian.

Location: Largo di Villa Peretti, 00185
Telephone Number: 00 39 06 3996 7700

Chapter Nine: Nightlife in Rome

Another best way to experience Rome is during night time. Rome offers a variety of choices on how to enjoy the night life that aren't just limited in going to clubs or bars. You can have lots of options where you can relax, enjoy and have the best time with your family. Rome turns into a very serene and romantic place at night so you can surely enjoy it with your loved one.

Here are 10 different places where you can spend the night while you are the Eternal City.

1. Piazza Navona and Via della Pace

The Piazza Navona and Via della Pace is an area in Rome that is famous for its nightlife for both tourists and locals alike. You can enjoy Rome's finest wine bars and authentic Italian cuisine. After which you can explore the labyrinth of alleys famous for its ancient looking cobblestone streets. Take a walk at this famous square or just chill with friends and family after a long day of sightseeing.

This area is best suited for friends and families who just want to spend the night and marvel at the historical places nearby or perhaps a quick chitchat with locals.

Here are the restaurants and coffee shops around Piazza Navona and Via della Pace. Warning: Pizza restaurants are everywhere!

- **La Focaccia**

  Location: Via della Pace, 11, 00186 Roma, Italy

  Tel. No: +39 06 9761 7557

  Opening Hours: 12PM–12:30AM

- **Cybo Restaurant**

  Location: Via di Tor Millina, 27, 00186 Roma, Italy

  Tel. No: +39 06 6821 0341

  Opening Hours: 10AM–2AM

- **Mami**

  Location: Via della Pace, 27A, 00186 Roma, Italy

  Tel. No: +39 06 4544 5543

  Opening Hours: 10:30AM–10PM

- **Navona Notte**

  Location: Via del Teatro Pace, 44, 00186 Roma, Italy

  Tel. No: +39 06 686 9278

- **Antica Trattoria della Pace**

  Location:Via della Pace, 1, 00186 Roma, Italy

  Tel. No: +39 06 683 8950

2. San Lorenzo

This is the place where younger generations hang out at night since it is near Italy's main university. You can of course, expect a lot of pubs, clubs and bars around the area. If you want to check out how the future generation of Rome is partying like a true Roman then better spend your night here!

Here are the bars and clubs around San Lorenzo. Warning: Young Romans and Italians everywhere!

- **Serpente pub**
  Location: Via dei Marsi, 21, 00185 Roma, Italy
  Tel. No: +39 06 490 9463

- **Bar dei Brutti**
  Location: Via dei Volsci, 71-73, 00185 Roma, Italy
  Tel. No: +39 06 8901 3825
  Opening Hours: 2PM – 2AM

- **Rive Gauche**
  Location: Via dei Sabelli, 43, 00185 Roma, Italy
  Tel. No: +39 06 445 6722
  Opening Hours: 7PM–2AM

- **Bar Marani**
  Location: Via dei Volsci, 57, 00185 Roma, Italy
  Tel. No: +39 06 490016

- **Victorian Monkey**

  Location:Via dello Scalo Di San Lorenzo 57, 00185

  Roma, Italy

  Tel. No: +39 06 9432 1895

  Opening Hours: 4:30PM–2AM

3. *Campo de Fiori*

For first time tourists or for visitors who are looking for something loud and fun then Campo de Fiori is the place for you! You can meet fellow tourists and of course you'll never run out of locals as well as drinks! The seemingly boring but great historical site turns into a place full of Romans partying and jamming with poetic tunes at night! This is the perfect place for mild - partying, bring you're A – game on because the drinks are on Rome!

Here are the bars and clubs around San Lorenzo. Warning: People partying partially are everywhere!

- **The Drunken Ship**
  Location: Piazza Campo de' Fiori, 20/21, 00186 Roma, Italy
  Tel. No: +39 06 6830 0535
  Opening Hours: 3PM–3AM

- **Open Baladin**
  Location: Via degli Specchi, 6
  Opening Hours: 12pm-1am

- **Coda di Gallo**
  Location: Via del Pellegrino, 13
  Opening Hours: 10pm-5am

- **Argot**
Location: Via dei Cappellari, 93
Opening Hours: Tue-Sat, 11pm-4am; Sun 11pm-12midnight

- **The Deer Club**
Location: Via Giulia, 131 (Hotel D.O.M.)
Opening Hours: 7pm-2am

4. *Trastevere*

This is another nightlife hotspot and center of social life in Rome famous for its bars and restaurants, and of course its awesome neighborhood. If you want to taste the best cocktails, wine and beer that Rome has to offer, then don't forget to drop by in Trastevere at night. Since this is one of Rome's nightlife centers, expect to meet lots of young Romans. The bars are always packed; the drinks and food are amazing and the scenery at night is just outstanding.

Here are the bars and restaurants around Trastevere. Warning: When you are in Trastevere, drink like a Roman!

Bar San Calisto

Location: Bar San Calisto, Piazza di San Calisto 4, Rome, Italy

Tel. No: +39 06 583 5869

Ma Che Siete Venuti a Fà

Location: Ma Che Siete Venuti a Fà, Via di Benedetta 25, Rome, Italy

Tel. No: +39 06 6456 2046

Freni e Frizioni

Location: Via del Politeama 4/6, Rome, Italy

Tel. No: +39 06 4549 7499

Niji

Location: Niji, Via dei Vascellari 35, Rome, Italy

Tel. No: +39 06 581 9520

Baylon Café

Location: Babylon Café, Via di San Francesco a Ripa 151

Tel. No: +39 06 581 4275

5. *Piazza Montvecchio*

If you are getting restless after a day full of historic trips, you can go to Piazza Montevecchio for a night full of fun! Grab one of Rome's best mojitos paired with a delicious Italian crusted pizza. The place is famous for its laid back yet artsy drinks and artisanal pizzas, so if you are craving for a light midnight snack, this is the perfect place to be. This is also a renowned place for casual dining and there are also pubs near the area and other local piazzas or squares you can go to. The restaurants around the area also offer international cuisines.

Here are the bars and restaurants around Piazza Montevecchio. Warning: Laid – back drinking is advised after a long trip down memory lane!

- **Ristorante Montevecchio**
  Location: Piazza Montevecchio, 22/a 00186 Roma, Italy
  Tel. No: +39 06 686 1319

- **No.au**
  Location: Piazza di Montevecchio, 16, 00186 Roma, Italy

- **Bar Del Fico**
  Location: Piazza del Fico, 26, 00186 Roma, Italy
  Tel. No: +39 06 6889 1373
  Opening Hours: 7:30AM–2AM

- **Obicà – Parlamento**
  Location: Piazza di Firenze, 28, 00186 Roma, Italy
  Tel. No: +39 06 683 2630
  Opening Hours: 8AM–12AM

- **Cul de Sac**

  Location: Piazza di Pasquino, 73, 00186 Roma, Italy

  Tel. No: +39 06 6880 1094

  Opening Hours: 12PM–12:30AM

6. *Piazza delle Copelle*

For real hardcore party – goers who wanted to have fun and dance the night away, Piazza delle Copelle is highly recommended for you. There are only a few clubs around the area – only reserve for those who are literally good at partying! So if you wanted to be seen and heard this is the go – to place for party people. Don't forget to bring your friends or loved ones with you and check out at some clubs around Piazza delle Copelle and spend a great night in the Eternal City! You can also check out the fine dining restaurants around the area.

Here are the bars and restaurants around Piazza delle Copelle. Warning: Party like a Roman gladiator!

- **Club Derrière**
  Location: Via delle Coppelle, 59, 00186 Roma, Italy
  Tel. No: +39 393 566 1077
  Opening Hours: 10PM–4AM

- **Osteria delle Coppelle**
  Location: Piazza delle Coppelle, 55/56/57, 00186 Roma, Italy
  Tel. No: +39 06 4550 2826
  Opening Hours: 12:30–4PM, 7PM–2AM

7. Monte Testaccio

Roman ships unloaded their cargos containing olive oil and wines at the river port which is now known today as Testaccio. The district is now also one of the centers of nigh life in Rome particularly on the weekends. The base of the hill that was once wine cellars are now filled with bars and restaurants, trattorias still exist around the area. Locals love to come here for its variety of clubs including a disco bar, a historic gay club, and also casual dining restaurants. They also offer the best wine in Rome.

Here are the bars and restaurants around Monte Testaccio. Warning: This place is probably where drinking started!

- **Goth-tinged Akab**
  Location: Via di Monte Testaccio 68

  Tel. No: +39 06 5725 0585

  Opening Hours: Tue-Fri

- **Coyote**
  Location: Via di Monte Testaccio 48B

  Tel. No: +39 340 241 2074

  Open daily

- **L'Alibi**
  Location: Via di Monte Testaccio 40

  Tel. No: +39 06 574 3448

  Open from Wed-Sat

*Most of these places open around 10.30pm and go on until 4 or 5 in the morning.

8. Piazza degli Aurunci

Piazza degli Aurunci is a place bustling with different nightlife scenes; you can enjoy drinking and eating inexpensive beers and food around the neighborhood. The place resembles a residential area and it is also near a night market. The crowds are usually dominated with young locals and young professionals. There are also lots of tattoo shops as well as occasional political conventions, music scene, open – mic nights and poetry readings.

You can immediately sense a friendly vibe around the area because it's a small neighborhood. Here are the bars and restaurants around Piazza degli Aurunci. Warning: If you are not into arts, go somewhere else!

- **Gente di S.Lorenzo**
  Location: Via degli Aurunci, 42-48, 00185 Roma, Italy
  Tel. No: +39 06 445 4425

- **Farinè la pizza**
  Location: Via degli Aurunci, 6, 00185 Roma, Italy
  Tel. No: +39 06 445 1162
  Opening Hours: 7:30–11:45PM

- **Giufà Libreria caffè**
  Location: Via degli Aurunci, 38, 00185 Roma, Italy
  Tel. No: +39 06 4436 1406
  Opening Hours: 10AM–12AM

- **TirAbouchon**
  Location: Via degli Aurunci, 26, 00185 Roma, Italy
  Tel. No: +39 349 159 6458
  Opening Hours: 7PM–3AM

9. EUR District

The EUR District in Rome is the center when it comes to clubbing; it's also where famous international DJs perform. It is boasting with good drinks, good food and great time! The place usually holds various events at night so if you wanted to continue partying like a Roman not just with locals but with other international guests, then better come to this place. The clubs are all worth it, this is perfect for tourists who wanted to splurge and just have a great time in this former glorious empire.

Here are the clubs around EUR District. Warning: This is the place where DJs and dancers collide!

- **Spazio Novecento**
  Location: Piazza Guglielmo Marconi, 26/b, 00144 Roma, Italy
  Tel. No: +39 06 5422 1107
  Opening Hours: 10AM–6PM

- **Futurarte**
  Location: Viale della Civiltà del Lavoro, 50/52, 00144 Roma, Italy
  Tel. No: +39 335 607 7922
  Opening Hours: 6:30AM–4PM

- **Jet Set**
  Location: Piazza di Spagna, Roma, Italy

10. *Piazza Bologna*

Another nightlife hotspot with young crowds around is Piazza Bologna. It is near the Sapienza University so expect to see lots of students around the area. The famous piazza is a commonplace for young people to chill out, drink and chitchat throughout the night. There are lots of cheap drinks, and trendy bar places around the area, as well as casual restaurants and coffee shops. Students also live around the neighborhood. Don't forget to bring your friends so you guys can meet a few Roman acquaintances

Here are the restaurants around Piazza Bologna. Warning: Millennials are all over the place - welcome to the 21st century Rome!

- **La Stiva**

  Location: Vl. Provincie, 56/58, 00162 Roma, Italy

  Tel. No: +39 06 4424 5237

  Opening Hours: 8:30AM–3:30PM, 6–11PM

- **Enrico A Piazza Bologna**

  Location: Via Michele di Lando, 28/36, 00162 Roma, Italy

  Tel. No: +39 06 4423 7738

  Opening Hours: 12:30–3PM, 7:30–11PM

- **Ristorante Senba**

  Location: Via Padova, 55, 00161 Roma, Italy

  Tel. No: +39 06 3105 0875

  Opening Hours: 12AM–3:30PM, 6PM–12AM

- **Stazione Cibo**

  Location: Largo Ravenna, 10, 00161 Roma, Italy

  Tel. No: +39 366 144 5570

  Opening Hours: 11AM–10PM

- **Trattoria da Neno**
  Location: Via Ravenna, 30, 00161 Roma, Italy
  Tel. No: +39 06 4429 0319
  Opening Hours: 8AM–1AM

Chapter Ten: Off - Beaten Path in Rome

Going off track in Rome is one of the things you should definitely try and do because aside from the fact that the places are not crowded with tourists, it's a great way to discover the hidden city behind its already glorious façade. Going to Rome's uncharted territories will make you discover more on why this city became the birthplace of the greatest civilization in history. This is perfectly suited for adventure seekers out there! Why not become Indiana Jones for a day in one of the coolest places in the world?

Here are top 10 off - beaten paths that you should see for yourself so you can look at the Eternal City from a different perspective.

1. Calcata

The great thing about Calcata is that it does not only have great scenery but it is also near a community of artists. The place is surrounded by green forests where you can find a cliff made out of volcanic rocks.

The village of Calcata was almost abandoned back in the day because of the stability issues of its location. However, around the 1960's Roman artists began to live and purchase a property around the area; eventually it was restored and became the place it is today.

This is best suited for people who wanted to take a break from the hustle and bustle of the city and all its historical sites. In Calcata you can enjoy getting lost in its labyrinth of streets and alleys as well as wander around the environmentally rich place. You should also stop by this place around the holidays where it is packed with people so that you'll witness the village's spirit. It's also highly recommended to talk and connect with the locals especially if you are a fellow artist yourself, who knows you might find a mentor here or the place could serve as an inspiration for your artistic passions.

2. *Tivoli: Villa d'Este*

Tivoli is about 30 km from Rome's city centre, the good news is that it can be easily reached through riding a bus or train. This small town is jam-packed with natural parks, Renaissance – old Villas, awesome gardens and another must – see historical site: the rural retreat house of Emperor Adriano.

This town is also famous for its thermal baths, in fact the smell of the sulfurous water from Tivoli sometimes reach Rome. You can visit a place called Villa d'Este which is a village owned by the family of Este, they are wealthy and famous aristocrats in Rome. The mansion and its jaw – dropping garden are now part of the UNESCO world heritage list.

The garden has allegorical fountains, pools and cascades. The water is supplied by the Aniene River without using mechanical pumps. The garden is built over a slope, and you can climb up the several terraces where you can oversee the city of Rome.

If you want to go to an interesting place packed with a fair amount of great sights and a cool neighborhood that is outside the city – centre then this is the place for you.

3. *Villa Gregoriana*

Villa Gregoriana is also located in Tivoli; the only difference of this compound compared to Villa d'Este is that it is more environmentally inclined.

Villa Gregoriana has luxurious vegetation along the steep slopes of the valley. The river of Aniene caused several floods back in the day which is why Pope Gregorious XVI ordered the park to be restored around the 19th century. The track of the river was eventually transformed into a romantic garden.

Villa Gregoriana sunk down for a long time until it was reopened for public less than 10 years ago. It brought the villa back to its original splendor. On top of the park, you can also see the ancient ruins of the temples from the Roman Acropolis.

This place is best suited for lovers and couples out there who wanted to have a romantic getaway or for tourists who wanted to enjoy scenery.

4. Anzio

Rome is not famous for its beaches and waters but like in any other countries, locals also need to soak and enjoy in the beach especially during summer. Anzio is the best place to go to if you is craving for a deep sea experience or if you wanted to wander around caves, cliffs and Roman ruins.

After enjoying the beach you can stroll around various WWF nature reserve called Tor Caldara, which is about 8 km from Anzio. The place is known for its fish economy. The town of Anzio is a small town where you can also connect with locals and be cave explorers or pirates for a day. This place is perfect for families who are looking to enjoy the waters of Rome without missing out the fun of exploration.

5. *Genzano*

Genzano is another small town near Rome that is away from tourist spots. This town is situated on the edge of a volcanic lake called Lago di Nemi. You can also check out its various historical centers spread out through its cobbled streets and tiny alleys. However, the main reason why you should drop by in Genzano is because of a religious event called Infiorata di Genzano. This even happens every year in the month of June during the Corpus Domini celebration. It lasts from Saturday to Monday.

This local festivity happens in one of the town's main street wherein it is covered with lots of flowers that usually represents civil or religious scenes. Usually the last day of the event ends with a parade in traditional costumes, after that kids are allowed to destroy the carpet of flowers and starts a petal fight! You can never find this kind of event anywhere in the world!

6. *Lago della Duchessa*

The Lago della Duchessa literally means the Lake of Duchess. It is a great destination if you want to go hiking. The best part is that it is not that far from the city center. It is beautiful a mountain lake with a great view and an altitude of about 1,788 meters above sea level. You can hike in Lago della Duchessa during summer or during winter. It's a pretty easy climb and it's perfect even for first time hikers.

After going to the lake you can immediate go back to the main city since it is near Rome and there are several buses that can take you back in no time after a day of trekking. Don't forget to eat an Italian pizza!

7. *Lago del Turano*

The Lago del Turano is a manmade lake that was built in 1939. It was once a reservoir for a hydroelectric plant. Today, Romans come here for a summer trip. You can relax and bathe under the sun on the lake's shores.

You can also check out the neighboring villages of Castel di Tora and Colle di Tora. It has small alleys and terraces where you can overlook the lake's amazing view.

The place is perfect for tourists who just wanted to chill and pretty much just do nothing for the day. You can enjoy a great local pizza paired with beers and a good time with your family or friends.

8. Allumiere

Allumiere is named after potassium – aluminum that was extracted from local mines. It is yet another perfect spot for trekking. It is actually a flat track following a railway that was blocked by a landslide back in 1961. The rails have been removed but tourists still use the track's markings for them to not get lost. It's a great trekking place because it has an unusual path, along the way you can see former train stations, a tunnel with a micro – climate and fauna as well as a metal bridge wherein you can pass through.

This place is also perfect for cyclists who wanted to travel long distances since the route is flat and you can follow the railway track. You can start your 50km journey in Monteromano and end up in Civitavecchia.

9. *Cerveteri*

If you wanted to get away from all the historical sites of the Roman Empire, you may want to check out the civilization that existed before Rome! It is called the Etruscan civilization which was formerly located in the north of Latium and in the south of Tuscany.

The Cerveteri is another UNESCO heritage site which contains the Necropolis of the Banditaccia. It is a complex that comprises over 1,000 tombs from the 9th century B.C. The graves are mound shaped, and some of it can also be found undergrounds with several levels. The main gem in the Necropolis is the Tomb of the Reliefs that dates back around 3rd century B.C. it is decorated with frescoes that depicts the contemporary life. You can learn more about the historical information of the place and the Etruscan population using a 3D video that is available inside the Cerveteri.

This place is perfect for those who wanted to discover more information about how Rome came about and for those who are seeking for a different kind of adventure and historical experience.

10. Gladiator Schools

I'm sure by this time you are all fed up with all of Rome's historical and religious sites – not to mention the artifacts and relics you have to endure and enjoy at the same time. You may also think that after reading about Rome's top tourist destinations including off – the – beaten – paths and its vibrant nightlife hotspots, you have probably seen the best that Rome has to offer. Well, I beg to differ. This last place is arguably one of the best experiences that you can ever have in the Eternal City.

When you talk about Rome, three main things come to mind – the Pope, the Roman Empire, and Gladiators!

Gladiators are without a doubt Rome's main legacy in world history. Sure you have heard the Spartans, and other fearless and brilliant army of other empires and civilizations but I'm sure we can all agree that the Romans are the best fighters that this world will ever know. Gladiators are sort of like the X – men breed and the Avengers in ancient times. This is like Kung Fu in China, it's a skill that every Roman has to master or at least learn in their lifetime.

They are not really soldiers or part of an army, being a gladiator is not also about who's the biggest, the strongest, the most skilled, the most talented or the most trained warrior - being a gladiator during the ancient Roman times are someone who has a strong heart and a fearless mind.

The best part is, you don't have to enter an arena and fight your way to the death against fearless warriors and strong beasts; you can learn how to become a gladiator by simply signing up in gladiator class and become a great warrior in just a few hours! Right in the center of all the action, the city that created the gladiator craze, and the place where watching humans kill one another for glory is completely acceptable and celebrated – none other than Rome!

There are also lots of other gladiator venues in Rome today that also offers "training" classes for kids and adults. Of course, the training will not be complete without the gladiator's armor, replicas of ancient Roman weaponry, a mini – arena, a Roman trainer, and a view of the Colosseum where real gladiators fight to the death thousands of years ago. The original Gladiator School is located in the famous Via Appia Antica – where the most famous ancient Roman gladiators were crucified.

Aside from the gladiator training, you will also get to handle some of the ancient items worn and used by real life gladiators centuries ago! How cool is that? Prices are not that expensive, and based on many tourists and locals who have experience gladiator classes, it's really worth it!

The place is run by Gruppo Storico Romano who is composed of Italian men and women addicted to ancient Rome's heritage which inspired them to teach others about their ancestor's most celebrated event. The spirit of Rome's greatest and fearless gladiators is waiting for you! Don't let this opportunity pass you by, so you can be part of the fiercest and legendary warriors in history.

Quick Travel Guide

The Eternal City will indeed last forever! Its grandiose manmade attractions, historical landmarks, ancient beginnings, faithful devotees, and the city's awesome descendants will truly make you remember their glorious past, appreciate their present and share the vision of their future. Enough has been said throughout this book for the city of God, so if you wanted to see and experience it for yourself, then what are you waiting for? Start packing your bags now and don't forget this book!

Visit the place where it all began, experience the phenomenal power of the Roman Empire that still echoes to this day, embody the spirit of a true Roman gladiator, taste the authentic Italian pizza and pasta and of course connect with God so you can come back home a different man!

Before this comes to an end, this chapter will provide you a quick travel guide. This contains the summary of all the places you've just read through as well as the necessary information that you need before traveling to Rome.

Remember all roads lead to Rome! *Viaggio felice! (Happy Trip)*

1. Rome Quick Facts

a. **Currency** – Leu or Lei (RON)

b. **Primary Language spoken:** Italian, English, Old Romanian Dialect

c. **Weather and seasons:** it has 4 seasons

- **Spring:** between March and mid – April; has a relatively mild and rainy season. The last few weeks of April and the month of May have warmer days but the sea breeze keeps it cool.

- **Summer:** between June to August; July being the hottest month with an average temperature of 26°C (78°F). It can go up to 34 °C - 38 °C. The temperature in the Roman coast can be cooler than the city center.

  - **Autumn:** usually between September to November. The temperature is mild and humid, with alternate periods of cloudy skies and occasional rains especially around the month of October. Frequent rains may begin in the last few weeks of November and the temperatures will also begin to drop for winter.

  - **Winter:** between December to February. The coldest is January; the temperature can easily drop to 8°C (46°F) or even at 7.5 °C. December is the wettest month in Rome; the city usually experiences an average of 96 mm of rain.

2. Transportation

Transportation Services in Rome

- Airplane
- Train (Domestic and International)
- Buses (Main City and Remote Places)
- Taxi/Uber

- Car Rental

3. *Travel Essentials*

Immigration and Visas

- If you are a tourist, you need to have a passport with 6 months of validity. A Schengen Visa may be required in some countries not included in the list (see list in Chapter 2). You can check out the consular website of Italy (see Visa and Passport Requirements Section) for more info.

Money Exchange

- The currency in Rome is called Leu or Lei. You may want to exchange your national money to any banks/money exchanger in Rome's capital - Bucharest.

ATMs and Credit Cards

- ATMs are found almost everywhere and are available 24/7.
- Credit cards such as American Express, Visa and MasterCard are accepted in various hotels,

restaurants, and shops except faraway places or remote places.

Electric and Voltage

- Rome's standard electrical voltage is 230 volts AC (50 cycles).

Communication Services

- You may rent a cell phone while you are in the city to make local or international calls easily. You may also opt to open your roaming services, although the charges will be a bit expensive (overseas charges) if you send international SMS or calls. Telephone booths still exist in the city but you need to buy a telephone card for you to make calls.

- The Wi-Fi and internet services in Rome are fast and accessible, although in some places such as remote areas or villages, access may be limited. Internet cafes and hotels are also offering high – speed internet access but you may need to pay for it to rent the computers.

Rome Highlights

1.) Where to Stay

Here's a quick list of the districts in Rome where you can stay during your trip.

- Centro - Storico
- Tridente
- Via Veneto and Villa Borghese
- Monti and the Celian Hill
- Testaccio and the Aventine Hill
- Trastevere
- Prati
- Ostia
- Campo de' Fiori and the Ghetto
- Vatican City

2.) Where to Eat

Here's a quick list of the foods you need to try in Rome.

- Cucina Romana
- Pizza

- Fine Dining
- Jewish Classics
- Street Food
- Gelato and Pastries
- Coffee Bars
- Wine and Cocktails
- Cheeses and Meats
- European Cuisines

3.) Tourists Spots

Here's a quick list of the famous tourist destinations in Rome:

- Roman Forum (Foro Romano)
- Ostia Antica
- The Pantheon
- Palatine Hill (Palatino)
- Trevi Fountain (Fontana di Trevi)
- The Spanish Steps (Scalinata della Trinità dei Monti)
- Hadrian's Villa (Villa Adriana)
- Pyramid of Cestius

- Ancient Appian Way (Via Appia Antica)

- The Colosseum (Colosseo)

4.) Churches in Rome

Here's a quick list of the churches and basilicas you can visit while in Rome:

- St. Peter's Basilica (Basilica di San Pietro in Vaticano)

- St. John Lateran (San Giovanni in Laterano)

- Basilica di Santa Maria Maggiore

- St. Peter in Chains (San Pietro in Vincoli)

- Santa Maria sopra Minerva

- Santa Maria del Popolo

- San Clemente

- Santa Maria in Cosmedin

- Santa Maria in Trastevere

- Santa Sabina

5.) Museums in Rome

Here's a quick list of the famous museums you can go to while you are in Rome.

- Museum of the Ara Pacis
- Borghese Gallery
- Capitoline Museums
- Centrale Montemartini
- Doria Pamphilj Gallery
- Maxxi Museum
- Museum and Crypt of the Capuchins
- Museo della Civiltà Romana
- Palazzo Altemps
- Palazzo Massimo alle Terme

6.) Nightlife in Rome

Here's a quick list of the places you can hang out at night in Rome.

- Piazza Navona and Via della Pace
- San Lorenzo

- Campo de Fiori

- Trastevere

- Piazza Montvecchio

- Piazza delle Copelle

- Monte Testaccio

- Piazza degli Aurunci

- EUR District

- Piazza Bologna

7.) Off – Beaten Path in Rome

Here's a quick list of the unchartered territories you can explore in Rome.

- Calcata

- Tivoli: Villa d'Este

- Tivoli: Villa Gregoriana

- Anzio

- Genzano

- Lago della Duchessa

- Lago del Turano

- Allumiere

- Cerveteri

- Gladiator School

PHOTO REFERENCES

Page Photo by user Skylark Pixabay.com,
https://pixabay.com/en/vittorio-emanuele-monument-rome-298412/

Page Photo by user Walkerssk Pixabay.com,
https://pixabay.com/en/rome-the-vatican-italy-1945033/

Page Photo by user TravelCoffeeBook Pixabay.com,
https://pixabay.com/en/vatican-rome-st-peters-basilica-594612/

Page Photo by user Terminals & Gates Flickr.com,
https://www.flickr.com/photos/terminals/13361563673/

Page Photo by user J Aaron Farr Flickr.com,
https://www.flickr.com/photos/jaaronfarr/519948326/in/photolist

Page Photo by user The_Double_A Pixabay.com,
https://pixabay.com/en/rome-colosseum-road-roman-coliseum-2030648/

Page Photo by user The_Double_A Pixabay.com,
https://pixabay.com/en/rome-italy-ancient-rome-2008387/

Page Photo by user kirkandmimi Pixabay.com,
https://pixabay.com/en/rome-italy-victor-emmanuel-1912715/

Page Photo by user 1103862 Pixabay.com,
https://pixabay.com/en/rome-spanish-steps-architecture-881633/

Page Photo by user xlizziexx Pixabay.com,
https://pixabay.com/en/villa-borghese-roma-rome-italy-537945/

Page Photo by user ohbendorf Pixabay.com,
https://www.flickr.com/photos/41994141@N08/5981907115/

Page Photo by user Nicola Flickr.com,
https://www.flickr.com/photos/15216811@N06/10387101306/

Page Photo by user Mario Sanchez Prada Flickr.com,
https://www.flickr.com/photos/mariosp/32879152691/

Page Photo by user Stefano Petroni Flickr.com,
https://www.flickr.com/photos/airforceone/4968319663/

Page Photo by user Stefano Corso Flickr.com, https://www.flickr.com/photos/pensiero/303356011/

Page Photo by user Cristian Viarisio Flickr.com, https://www.flickr.com/photos/tesking/1303675439/

Page Photo by user kirkandmimi Pixabay.com, https://pixabay.com/en/rome-st-peters-saint-peters-vatican-2261190/

Page Photo by user Julen Landa Flickr.com, https://www.flickr.com/photos/txanoduna/6357130281/

Page Photo by user Fabio De angeli Flickr.com, https://www.flickr.com/photos/151196503@N02/31988624100/

Page Photo by user Ernesto Andrade Flickr.com, https://www.flickr.com/photos/dongkwan/6774513359/

Page Photo by user Tavallai Flickr.com, https://www.flickr.com/photos/tavallai/6970982950/

Page Photo by user Diego Flickr.com, https://www.flickr.com/photos/dags1974/15959563240/

Page Photo by user Stephen Bugno Flickr.com, https://www.flickr.com/photos/52442953@N05/8407831045/

Page Photo by user kirkandmimi Pixabay.com, https://pixabay.com/en/rome-roma-italy-cafe-italian-1968149/

Page Photo by user Stefano Constantini Flickr.com, https://www.flickr.com/photos/stefanorometours/8482523138/

Page Photo by user Kurt Flickr.com, https://www.flickr.com/photos/kwilms/847524091/

Page Photo by user sharonang Pixabay.com, https://pixabay.com/en/tomato-coffee-cafe-lunch-food-1204651/

Page Photo by user serghei_topor Pixabay.com, https://pixabay.com/en/the-altar-of-the-fatherland-760337/

Page Photo by user ScapinPixabay.com, https://pixabay.com/en/rome-italy-antique-roman-forum-944852/

Page Photo by user neufal54 Pixabay.com,
https://pixabay.com/en/italy-ostia-antica-ruins-1314573/

Page Photo by user kirkandmimi Pixabay.com,
https://pixabay.com/en/rome-pantheon-piazza-rotonda-2027876/

Page Photo by user Melissa Delzio Flickr.com,
https://www.flickr.com/photos/melissadelzio/6963556645/

Page Photo by user skylark Pixabay.com,
https://pixabay.com/en/trevi-fountain-fontana-di-trevi-rome-298411/

Page Photo by user Seneca Pixabay.com,
https://pixabay.com/en/spanish-steps-rome-stairs-building-84181/

Page Photo by user Elizabeth Buie Flickr.com,
https://www.flickr.com/photos/ebuie/3672037958/

Page Photo by user Giorgio Rodano Flickr.com,
https://www.flickr.com/photos/134205948@N02/24935165646/

Page Photo by user Herb Neufeld Flickr.com,
https://www.flickr.com/photos/oggiedog/6216393290/

Page Photo by user TreptowerAlex Flickr.com,
https://pixabay.com/en/colosseum-rome-italy-romans-1014310/

Page Photo by user moisemarian Flickr.com,
https://pixabay.com/en/rome-statue-sculpture-architecture-1761928/

Page Photo by user Tama66 Pixabay.com,
https://pixabay.com/en/apostle-bible-rome-1701732/

Page Photo by user Juan Salmoral Flickr.com,
https://www.flickr.com/photos/juanillooo/407766838/

Page Photo by user Gyorgy Soponvai Flickr.com,
https://www.flickr.com/photos/vanamonde81/15310488801/in/photolist

Page Photo by user Robin Zebrowski Flickr.com,
https://www.flickr.com/photos/firepile/11932433674/

Page Photo by user Holly Hayes Flickr.com,
https://www.flickr.com/photos/sacred_destinations/5561365
975/

Page Photo by user Serquei Flickr.com,
https://www.flickr.com/photos/serguei2k/3843644938/in/pho
tolist

Page Photo by user Holly Hayes Flickr.com,
https://www.flickr.com/photos/sacred_destinations/3053598
644/

Page Photo by user Michiel Jeliis Flickr.com,
https://www.flickr.com/photos/thewolf/4122286824/

Page Photo by user Franz Jachim Flickr.com,
https://www.flickr.com/photos/franzj/4954753131/in/photolis
t

Page Photo by user Lawrence OP Flickr.com,
https://www.flickr.com/photos/paullew/5098413663/

Page Photo by user rebeccakiessling1 Flickr.com,
https://pixabay.com/en/romulus-remus-capitoline-wolf-
rome-1928153/

Page Photo by user Mzximvs VdB Flickr.com, https://www.flickr.com/photos/magnusmaximus/14514394706/

Page Photo by user Mark B. Schlemmer Flickr.com, https://www.flickr.com/photos/mbschlemmer/3122976776/

Page Photo by user dvdbramhall Flickr.com, https://www.flickr.com/photos/bramhall/11950140613/

Page Photo by user Carole Raddato Flickr.com, https://www.flickr.com/photos/carolemage/31781543494/

Page Photo by user damian entwistle Flickr.com, https://www.flickr.com/photos/damiavos/27781413716/

Page Photo by user Wojtek Gurak Flickr.com, https://www.flickr.com/photos/wojtekgurak/12922214674/

Page Photo by user stanthejeep Wikimedia Commons, https://commons.wikimedia.org/wiki/File:Capuchin_Crypt.jpg

Page Photo by user Stef Flickr.com, https://www.flickr.com/photos/stefz/114563099/

Page Photo by user dvdbramhall Flickr.com,
https://www.flickr.com/photos/bramhall/4290099501/in/photolist

Page Photo by user dvdbramhall Flickr.com,
https://www.flickr.com/photos/bramhall/11949150045/

Page Photo by user putative3 Pixabay.com,
https://pixabay.com/en/republica-rome-night-116011/

Page Photo by user Michael Foley Flickr.com,
https://www.flickr.com/photos/michaelfoleyphotography/5854172338/

Page Photo by user Aleteia Image Department Flickr.com,
https://www.flickr.com/photos/113018453@N05/14013352602/

Page Photo by user Ratio Partners Flickr.com,
https://www.flickr.com/photos/pmorgan67/2197211751/in/photolist

Page Photo by user Remy Frank Flickr.com,
https://www.flickr.com/photos/eldelfraval/15192320337/

Page Photo by user Sean Perry Flickr.com,
https://www.flickr.com/photos/niceguysean/21970506/

Page Photo by user Lalupa Flickr.com,
https://commons.wikimedia.org/wiki/File:S_Eustachio_-
_p_delle_coppelle_1180181.JPG

Page Photo by user telwink Flickr.com,
https://www.flickr.com/photos/telwink/4339629938/

Page Photo by user Fabio Stefano Alla Flickr.com,
https://www.flickr.com/photos/fabioalla/8350052976/

Page Photo by user Francisco Anzola Flickr.com,
https://www.flickr.com/photos/fran001/26967866753/

Page Photo by user Rodrigo Soldon Flickr.com,
https://www.flickr.com/photos/soldon/5347897588/

Page Photo by user Tommy Clark Flickr.com,
https://www.flickr.com/photos/tommyscapes/10108605765/

Page Photo by user Ken Flickr.com,
https://www.flickr.com/photos/draks/2109225704/in/photolis
t

Page Photo by user Pachelbel Canon Flickr.com,
https://www.flickr.com/photos/73154039@N00/33989761001/

Page Photo by user Herb Neufeld Flickr.com,
https://www.flickr.com/photos/oggiedog/6290105083/in/photolist

Page Photo by user Gianmaria M.Flickr.com,
https://www.flickr.com/photos/37895381@N05/3494852325/

Page Photo by user Ferdinando Chiodo Wikimedia Commons,
https://commons.wikimedia.org/wiki/File:Parco_Palazzo_Sforza_Cesarini.jpg

Page Photo by user Paolo De Santis RomeInsiderGuide.com,
http://www.romeinsiderguide.com/hikes-near-rome.html

Page Photo by user Altotemi Wikimedia Commons,
https://commons.wikimedia.org/wiki/File:Lago_del_turano.jpg

Page Photo by user Davide Vadala Pinterest.com,
https://goo.gl/images/3z2fQZ

Page Photo by user Romanus_too Flickr.com,
https://www.flickr.com/photos/11257308@N06/3754514135/

Page Photo by user Viator.com Flickr.com,
https://www.flickr.com/photos/viator-things-to-do/905162151/

Page Photo by user elukac Pixabay.com,
https://pixabay.com/en/horses-roman-arena-historic-race-1976554/

REFERENCES

10 Innovations that Built Ancient Rome – History.com

http://www.history.com/news/history-lists/10-innovations-that-built-ancient-rome

10 Off-the-Beaten Path Places in Rome – We3Travel.com

https://we3travel.com/10-off-the-beaten-path-places-in-rome/

10 of the best bars in Rome – The Guardian

https://www.theguardian.com/travel/2011/jul/13/top-10-bars-in-rome

10 of the best museums and galleries in Rome – The Guardian

https://www.theguardian.com/travel/2011/jul/13/top-10-museums-galleries-rome

10 Places to Eat Incredibly Well in Rome Italy – FoodRepublic.com

http://www.foodrepublic.com/2015/05/21/10-places-to-eat-incredibly-well-in-rome-italy/

15 Top-Rated Churches in Rome – Planetware.com

http://www.planetware.com/italy/top-rated-churches-in-rome-i-zzz-16.htm

About Rome – World Travel Guide

http://www.worldtravelguide.net/guides/europe/italy/rome/

A Brief History of Rome – Roman – Empire.net

http://www.roman-empire.net/children/history.html

A Brief History of Rome – thoughtco.com

https://www.thoughtco.com/brief-history-of-rome-1221658

An Expert's Guide: The Best Area to Stay in Rome – RoughGuides.com

https://www.roughguides.com/article/best-area-to-stay-in-rome/

Best Things to Do in Rome – USNews.com

http://travel.usnews.com/Rome_Italy/Things_To_Do/

Brief History of Rome – tribunesandtriumphs.org

http://www.tribunesandtriumphs.org/roman-empire/brief-history-of-rome.htm

Culture and Tradition in Rome, Italy – USAToday.com

http://traveltips.usatoday.com/culture-traditions-rome-italy-11465.html

Culture of Ancient Rome – Wikipedia.org

https://en.wikipedia.org/wiki/Culture_of_ancient_Rome

Entry Requirements & Customs – Frommers.com

http://www.frommers.com/destinations/rome/planning-a-trip/entry-requirements--customs

Go Off the Path with 10 Unusual Things To Do in Rome – Anglo-ItalianFollowus.com

http://www.angloitalianfollowus.com/unusual-things-to-do-in-rome

Greatest Ancient Roman Contributions – Eupedia.com

http://www.eupedia.com/forum/threads/20285-Greatest-Ancient-Roman-contribution(s)-to-the-world

Hikes near Rome – RomeInsiderGuide.com

http://www.romeinsiderguide.com/hikes-near-rome.html

Hotels in Rome – Hotels.com

https://ph.hotels.com/de712491/hotels-rome-italy

Is Rome Italy Considered Sub – Tropical – City-data.com

http://www.city-data.com/forum/weather/1218257-rome-italy-considered-sub-tropical.html

Italy at its Best – ItalyGuides.it

https://www.italyguides.it/en/

Italy Visa and Passport Requirements – World Travel Guide

http://www.worldtravelguide.net/guides/europe/italy/passport-visa/

Locals Reveal the Best Things To Do In Rome – BusinessInsider.com

http://www.businessinsider.com/locals-reveal-the-best-things-to-do-in-rome-2014-4

Names or Synonyms for Rome – Thoughtco.com

https://www.thoughtco.com/names-or-synonyms-for-rome-117755

Off the Beaten Path – 10 Amazing Places to See near Rome – ThePlanetd.com

http://theplanetd.com/off-the-beaten-path-10-amazing-places-to-see-near-rome/

Ostia Antica – Triphistoric.com

https://www.triphistoric.com/ostia-antica-339/

People – RomaniaTourism.com

http://romaniatourism.com/people.html

Proverbs, Quotes, and Sayings of Ancient Rome – Tentonhammer.com

http://www.tentonhammer.com/articles/proverbs-quotes-and-sayings-of-ancient-rome

Public Holidays in Rome – Rome.net

https://www.rome.net/holidays

Restaurants in Rome – CNTraveler.com

http://www.cntraveler.com/stories/2013-09-15/locals-favorites-restaurants-rome

Romania – Practical Information - RomaniaTourism.com

http://romaniatourism.com/practical-information.html

Rome – Wikitravel.org

http://wikitravel.org/en/Rome

Rome's best museums and art galleries – Telegraph UK

http://www.telegraph.co.uk/travel/destinations/europe/italy/rome/articles/Romes-best-museums-and-art-galleries/

Roman Empire – Wikipedia.org

https://en.wikipedia.org/wiki/Roman_Empire

Roman Empire Timeline – SoftSchools.com

http://www.softschools.com/timelines/roman_empire/timeline_9/

Roman Forum (Foro Romano) – USNews.com

http://travel.usnews.com/Rome_Italy/Things_To_Do/Roman_Forum_Foro_Romano_28759/

Roman History Timeline – West Chester University of Pennsylvania

http://courses.wcupa.edu/jones/his101/web/t-roman.htm

Rome in a Nutshell – ItalyGuides.it

https://www.italyguides.it/en/lazio/rome/travel-guides/travel-tips/rome-in-a-nutshell

Rome Italy Travel Guide – Rome.info

http://www.rome.info/

Rome nightlife – Telegraph UK

http://www.telegraph.co.uk/travel/destinations/europe/italy/rome/articles/rome-nightlife/

Rome Nightlife Guide – HungryPartier.com

https://hungrypartier.com/ultimate-guide-to-the-nightlife-in-rome/

Rome Nightlife Guide: NightClubs for Dancing – Romeing.it

http://www.romeing.it/rome-nightlife-guide-night-clubs/

Rome Tourist Info – Turismo Roma

http://www.turismoroma.it/?lang=en

Top 10 Most Stunning Roman Catholic Basilicas – Listverse.com

http://listverse.com/2009/05/22/top-10-most-stunning-roman-catholic-basilicas/

Tourist Attraction in Rome – TheMost10.com

http://www.themost10.com/tourist-attractions-in-rome/

Travel Advice for Italy – Rome.net

https://www.rome.net/entry-requirements

Trevi Fountain (Fontana di Trevi) – USNews.com

http://travel.usnews.com/Rome_Italy/Things_To_Do/Trevi_F
ountain_Fontana_di_Trevi_28758/

The Best Museums & Galleries in Rome to Visit? –
RomeToolKit.com

https://www.rometoolkit.com/whattodo/rome_museums.ht
ml

The Best Restaurants in Rome Tourists Don't Know About
– CnTraveler.com

http://www.cntraveler.com/stories/2013-09-15/locals-
favorites-restaurants-rome

**The Most Jaw Dropping Churches in Rome That Aren't
Called St. Peter's (A Pilgrimage to Rome Guide)** – Walks of
Italy

https://www.walksofitaly.com/blog/rome/the-most-jaw-
dropping-churches-in-rome-that-arent-called-st-peters-a-
pilgrimage-to-rome-guide

**The Legacy of Rome and What Have the Romans Done for
Us** – RomanFrontier.eu

http://www.romanfrontier.eu/en/about-limes/legacy-rome-
what-have-romans-done-us

The Story of the Roman Empire Full BBC Documentary – Youtube.com

https://www.youtube.com/watch?v=U-MxSmeLkJs&spfreload=10

The Top 10 Off-the-Beaten Path Spots in Rome – UntappedCities.com

http://untappedcities.com/2014/04/16/the-top-10-off-the-beaten-path-spots-in-rome/

Villa dei Quintili – Triphistoric.com

https://www.triphistoric.com/villa-dei-quintili-751/

Weather in Rome Italy – TimeandDate.com

https://www.timeanddate.com/weather/italy/rome

Worried about trying to interest kids in yet another ancient Roman monument? Rome's Gladiator School is the answer to your prayers! – Explore-Italian-culture.com

http://www.explore-italian-culture.com/gladiator-school.html

What to See in Rome - Top 10 Places to Visit – Triphistoric.com

https://www.triphistoric.com/what-to-see-in-rome/fr265

When in Rome, Eat like a Local – Momondo.com

http://www.momondo.com/inspiration/where-to-eat-in-rome/

Where to Eat & Drink in Rome in 2017 – Katieparla.com

http://katieparla.com/where-to-eat-drink-shop-rome/

Where to head in Rome when the sun goes down –
10best.com

http://www.10best.com/destinations/italy/rome/nightlife/best-nightlife/

Where to Stay in Rome – Rome.net

https://www.rome.net/where-to-stay

Feeding Baby
Cynthia Cherry
978-1941070000

Axolotl
Lolly Brown
978-0989658430

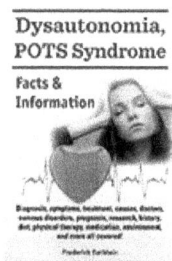

Dysautonomia, POTS
Syndrome
Frederick Earlstein
978-0989658485

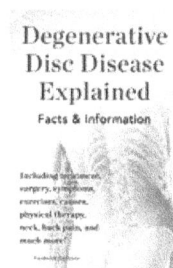

Degenerative Disc
Disease Explained
Frederick Earlstein
978-0989658485

Sinusitis, Hay Fever,
Allergic Rhinitis Explained
Frederick Earlstein
978-1941070024

Wicca
Riley Star
978-1941070130

Zombie Apocalypse
Rex Cutty
978-1941070154

Capybara
Lolly Brown
978-1941070062

Eels As Pets
Lolly Brown
978-1941070167

Scabies and Lice Explained
Frederick Earlstein
978-1941070017

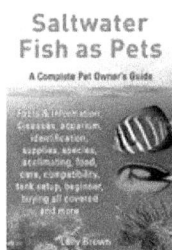

Saltwater Fish As Pets
Lolly Brown
978-0989658461

Torticollis Explained
Frederick Earlstein
978-1941070055

Kennel Cough
Lolly Brown
978-0989658409

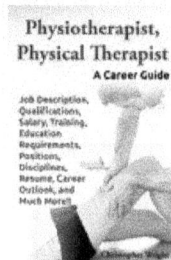

Physiotherapist, Physical
Therapist
Christopher Wright
978-0989658492

Rats, Mice, and Dormice
As Pets
Lolly Brown
978-1941070079

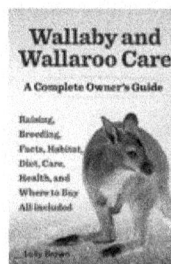

Wallaby and Wallaroo Car
Lolly Brown
978-1941070031

Bodybuilding Supplements Explained
Choosing The Correct Supplements

Bodybuilding Supplements
Explained
Jon Shelton
978-1941070239

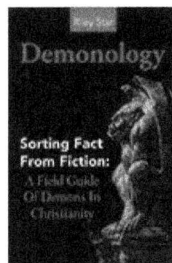

Demonology
Riley Star

Sorting Fact
From Fiction:
A Field Guide
Of Demons In
Christianity

Demonology
Riley Star
978-19401070314

Pigeon Racing
Facts & Information

Handling, health, keeping, housing,
breeding, racing, and training

Lolly Brown

Pigeon Racing
Lolly Brown
978-1941070307

Dwarf Hamster
How To Care For Your
Pet Dwarf Hamster

Lolly Brown

Dwarf Hamster
Lolly Brown
978-1941070390

Cryptozoology
Rex Cutty
978-1941070406

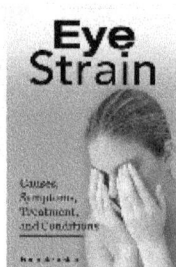

Eye Strain
Frederick Earlstein
978-1941070369

Inez The Miniature Elephant
Asher Ray
978-1941070353

Vampire Apocalypse
Rex Cutty
978-1941070321